THE PENGUIN POETS

WILLIAM BLAKE

WILLIAM BLAKE

A SELECTION OF POEMS AND LETTERS
EDITED WITH
AN INTRODUCTION BY

J. BRONOWSKI

PENGUIN BOOKS

Penguin Books Ltd, Harmondsworth, Middlesex, England
Penguin Books Inc., 7110 Ambassador Road, Baltimore, Maryland 21207, U.S.A.
Penguin Books Australia Ltd Ringwood, Victoria, Australia
Penguin Books Canada Ltd. 41 Steelcase Road West,
Markham, Ontario, Canada
Penguin Books (N.Z.) Ltd, 182–190 Wairau Road,
Auckland 10 New Zealand

—

This selection first published 1958
Reprinted 1961, 1964, 1965, 1966, 1968, 1970, 1971, 1972, 1973, 1975, 1976

—

Copyright © the Estate of J. Bronowski, 1958

—

Made and printed in Great Britain
by Cox & Wyman Ltd,
London, Reading and Fakenham
Set in Monotype Baskerville

CONTENTS

CONTENTS

CONTENTS

CONTENTS

INTRODUCTION

WILLIAM BLAKE was born in London on 28 November 1757, and died there on 12 August 1827. From childhood he had a strongly visual mind: whatever he imagined he also saw. His father apprenticed him to an engraver and by this craft he lived. He also drew and painted, but his work was not liked, and only in his last years was he given the chance to make the noble and original designs which had crowded his head all his life.

Blake wrote poems from the time that he was a boy: the friends who printed his first book, *Poetical Sketches*, said that it was 'the production of untutored youth, commenced in his twelfth, and occasionally resumed by the author till his twentieth year'. He went on writing first lyric and then prophetic poems, but they were not to the taste of his time, and when he wanted to print them he and his wife had to do so with their own hands. They were etched by Blake on small copper plates with pictures in the margins and printed and coloured one by one. On many pages the poem and the design are one, and no one cared for either.

There were several reasons for this neglect. As his letters show, Blake was a difficult man: odd and sensitive and single-minded at the same time. He was self-taught, so that his judgements were penetrating and childish by turns; he sometimes spoke as if no one had thought of the things he thought about. His visual imagination made everything that he said more than life-size, and as disturbing as a dream which is unreal because it is too real. He never tried in the least to fit into the world; simply, innocently, and completely, he was a rebel.

From the time of the American Revolution in 1775 to the rise of Napoleon after 1796, Blake was a rebel in the plainest way. He supported the American and French Revolutions, he praised Washington and Lafayette, he wrote against George III and the King of France, and he was one among the revolutionary friends of Tom Paine and Henry Fuseli and their publisher Joseph Johnson. All this can be read in the earlier prophetic books, such

9

as *America* and *The Song of Los*. And it ripples under the lucid surface of the lyric poems, where it makes the contrast between the *Songs of Innocence*, which were etched in the high hope of the French Revolution in 1789, and the *Songs of Experience*, which were etched when England and France were at war in 1794.

The years of war, however, made Blake's Radical politics more and more a handicap to him. His livelihood was hard hit by the slump of 1797. His more respectable friends, among them his patron Thomas Butts and the artist John Flaxman, wanted him to make a fresh start away from London. Blake was engraving for the books of the Liberal poet and bore William Hayley, and in 1800 he moved to Felpham in Sussex to work with Hayley. By this time Napoleon had turned the French Revolution into a tyranny, and Blake came to despair of it and of all politics. Nevertheless, his last act before he left Felpham in 1803 was to get into a dispute with a soldier, as a result of which he was tried for sedition. He was acquitted, but he had been frightened.

These events combined to change the form of Blake's intransigence. Some time between 1796 and 1800 the political undertone fades from his poems and their mood becomes more and more Christian. About this time, his imagery and his rhythms, for example in *Vala or the Four Zoas*, take on the biblical airs, the visionary warnings, and the unending swell which characterize his later poems. The two long prophetic books which Blake wrote after 1804, *Milton* and *Jerusalem*, have made this religious manner familiar.

These later poems have given Blake the reputation of a Christian hermit who lived remote from the world and was lost in his own mystic vision. The picture has some plausible touches. After his return to London Blake was more and more alone and poor, and lived by hack work. His prejudices against some kinds of painting and many kinds of science grew stronger, for the failure of his Radical hopes now made him suspicious of rational and material plans for human betterment. He attracted young men with saintly ideas, such as the painter John Linnell, and they kept him by commissioning his last and best designs, for Dante and for *The Book of Job*.

Yet this picture of Blake as a pious hermit is false. He was not like this at any time in his life, before or after 1800. He was and he remained robust, matter-of-fact, and a rebel. He is as downright a rebel in the later religious writings as in his early Radical ones.

Blake's form of Christianity was heretical, for it identified Christ the Son with all spiritual goodness and made God the Father a symbol of terror and tyranny. And this, the Gnostic or Manichaean heresy, is not merely a technical nicety among sects: it is a crux in Blake's mind. God to Blake personified absolute authority, and Christ personified the human character; and Blake was on the side of man against authority, at the end of his life when he called the authority Church and God, as much as at the beginning when he called it State and King. We can read this in the unfinished drafts of *The Everlasting Gospel* and in the indignant notes he wrote in his seventieth year on Dr Thornton's version of the Lord's Prayer. To Blake, all virtue is human virtue, and in his most religious poems he acknowledges no other Christianity.

> The Worship of God is honouring his gifts
> In other men & loving the greatest men best, each according
> To his Genius which is the Holy Ghost in Man; there is no other
> God than that God who is the intellectual fountain of Humanity.

This is the unity between the early Blake and the late, the Radical and the heretic, and it joins the lyric poems, whose meanings seem so much simpler than they are, to the tortuous and smoky rhetoric of the later prophetic books.

Blake wrote almost a quarter of a million words in his prophetic books. They were not careful and polished words; he wrote them as they came to him, and he did not always go back today over what he had written yesterday. So the prophetic books are constantly in movement and changing: the surface is alive, the thought is never still, and the symbols are never quite the same. The prophetic writings are an immense diary or commonplace book in which Blake wrote night after night much of what came into his head, in an endless commentary on his spiritual and physical life. They are the expression not of a system or point of view but of a whole personality; and under their constant changes, the personality and the subject are always the same. The subject is the distortion of man by the rigid frame of law and society and the conventional systems; and the triumph is always the liberation of man by his own energies. The subject is war, tyranny, and poverty; the triumph is human freedom. Under all the strangling proliferation of Blake's mythology this is the single theme, and it is expressed in two opposing characters. One is the jealous and fearful God of the Old Testament, oppressive in State and Church, whom Blake calls Urizen. The other is the perpetually young figure of Christ with the sword, overthrowing the established orders and bringing danger and liberty in his two hands. Blake first called this character Orc, and later divided him into two parts. One part is the male hero Los, who has to struggle with his own human failings as well as against Urizen. The other is Los's more cautious female counterpart Enitharmon, whose womanly shrinkings and whose tenderness to the natural world must be mastered before humanity can fulfil itself. And if men and women do not fulfil themselves, if they shirk experience, they are dead in spirit: this is already the theme of the early *Book of Thel*.

These figures and beliefs in Blake grew out of his own experience, on which he constantly drew. Los works at a forge and Enitharmon at a loom: they take their crafts from the Industrial Revolution, through which Blake lived. He saw its machinery grow round him and wrote about it and feared it; his own craft of engraving in the end was destroyed by the Industrial Revolution. His writings are full of sensible references to Malthus and the Poor Law and the news of the day, and the fact that he lived in Hercules Buildings and that the soldier with whom he scuffled was called John Scholfield. To Blake, the world of his poems was not a retreat from but an expansion of his everyday world.

It is the belief of imaginative poets that they are the symbol and the voice of universal experiences more lasting than the accidents of time. Their poetry speaks from one age to another, because it is founded in experiences which are simple, common, profound, which are human and universal. Such was the belief of Blake. But to his generation, the generation of Peterloo, the timeless human experiences did not end at love, beauty, truth and passion. They included war and repression, poverty and fear and injustice, the loss of place and the social disasters. Blake read in these the signs of all human longing, and gave them an imaginative force which makes them still vivid to our generation, the generation of Belsen, and which makes his writings a universal monument of the spirit.

In making this choice of Blake's work, I have wanted to present him as he was, a single person who did different things and did everything in his own way. Therefore I have not chosen only the poems which I like best or those which seem easiest to read. I have of course given the largest space to his lyric poems and, among his prophetic writings, to the earlier books such as *The Marriage of Heaven and Hell*. But Blake was a poet who wrote in two manners, and did so by design; and to ignore the more difficult manner in which he chose to write his later prophetic books (as of course every reader is tempted to do) would be an insult to him and a caricature of his work. The poet must be seen whole, and what is read of him should be a whole. In particular, one ought to print those of his books from which one quotes, whole; and this I have done wherever I could. But the later prophetic poems are of course too long, and instead I have tried to give their feeling and movement by quoting from each a single long, consecutive passage.

This book is not intended to give a view of Blake's prose writings, which make an interesting but different study. The one set of Blake's annotations and the few letters which I have put at the end have a simpler purpose. They are intended to give the reader at first hand something of the character of the man and the circumstances in which he worked; and if they succeed in doing this, they are the only footnotes which the book needs.

The poems of Blake and his prose writings have been edited with devoted scholarship by Geoffrey Keynes in volumes published by the Nonesuch Press. I have taken over his readings almost everywhere, and I am indebted to him and to the Nonesuch Library for letting me do so.

WILLIAM BLAKE

From POETICAL SKETCHES

To Spring

O Thou, with dewy locks, who lookest down
Thro' the clear windows of the morning; turn
Thine angel eyes upon our western isle,
Which in full choir hails thy approach, O Spring!

The hills tell each other, and the list'ning
Vallies hear; all our longing eyes are turned
Up to thy bright pavillions: issue forth,
And let thy holy feet visit our clime.

Come o'er the eastern hills, and let our winds
Kiss thy perfumed garments; let us taste
Thy morn and evening breath; scatter thy pearls
Upon our love-sick land that mourns for thee.

O deck her forth with thy fair fingers; pour
Thy soft kisses on her bosom; and put
Thy golden crown upon her languish'd head,
Whose modest tresses were bound up for thee!

To Morning

O Holy virgin! clad in purest white,
Unlock heav'n's golden gates, and issue forth;
Awake the dawn that sleeps in heaven; let light
Rise from the chambers of the east, and bring
The honied dew that cometh on waking day.
O radiant morning, salute the sun,
Rouz'd like a huntsman to the chace; and, with
Thy buskin'd feet, appear upon our hills.

Song

How sweet I roam'd from field to field,
  And tasted all the summer's pride,
'Till I the prince of love beheld,
  Who in the sunny beams did glide!

He shew'd me lilies for my hair,
  And blushing roses for my brow;
He led me through his gardens fair,
  Where all his golden pleasures grow.

With sweet May dews my wings were wet,
  And Phoebus fir'd my vocal rage;
He caught me in his silken net,
  And shut me in his golden cage.

He loves to sit and hear me sing,
  Then, laughing, sports and plays with me;
Then stretches out my golden wing,
  And mocks my loss of liberty.

Song

My silks and fine array,
  My smiles and languish'd air,
By love are driv'n away;
  And mournful lean Despair
Brings me yew to deck my grave:
Such end true lovers have.

His face is fair as heav'n,
  When springing buds unfold;
O why to him was't giv'n,
  Whose heart is wintry cold?
His breast is love's all worship'd tomb,
Where all love's pilgrims come.

Bring me an axe and spade,
   Bring me a winding sheet;
When I my grave have made,
   Let winds and tempests beat:
Then down I'll lie, as cold as clay.
True love doth pass away!

Mad Song

The wild winds weep,
   And the night is a-cold;
Come hither, Sleep,
   And my griefs infold:
But lo! the morning peeps
   Over the eastern steeps,
And the rustling birds of dawn
The earth do scorn.

Lo! to the vault
   Of paved heaven,
With sorrow fraught
   My notes are driven:
They strike the ear of night,
   Make weep the eyes of day;
They make mad the roaring winds,
   And with tempests play.

Like a fiend in a cloud
   With howling woe,
After night I do croud,
   And with night will go;
I turn my back to the east,
From whence comforts have increas'd;
For light doth seize my brain
With frantic pain.

To the Muses

Whether on Ida's shady brow,
  Or in the chambers of the East,
The chambers of the sun, that now
  From antient melody have ceas'd;

Whether in Heav'n ye wander fair,
  Or the green corners of the earth,
Or the blue regions of the air,
  Where the melodious winds have birth;

Whether on chrystal rocks ye rove,
  Beneath the bosom of the sea
Wand'ring in many a coral grove,
  Fair Nine, forsaking Poetry!

How have you left the antient love
  That bards of old enjoy'd in you!
The languid strings do scarcely move!
  The sound is forc'd, the notes are few!

Gwin, King of Norway

Come, Kings, and listen to my song,
  When Gwin, the son of Nore,
Over the nations of the North
  His cruel sceptre bore:

The Nobles of the land did feed
  Upon the hungry Poor;
They tear the poor man's lamb, and drive
  The needy from their door!

The land is desolate; our wives
  And children cry for bread;
Arise, and pull the tyrant down;
  Let Gwin be humbled!

Gordred the giant rous'd himself
   From sleeping in his cave;
He shook the hills, and in the clouds
   The troubl'd banners wave.

Beneath them roll'd, like tempests black,
   The num'rous sons of blood;
Like lions' whelps, roaring abroad,
   Seeking their nightly food.

Down Bleron's hills they dreadful rush,
   Their cry ascends the clouds;
The trampling horse, and clanging arms
   Like rushing mighty floods!

Their wives and children, weeping loud,
   Follow in wild array,
Howling like ghosts, furious as wolves
   In the bleak wintry day.

'Pull down the tyrant to the dust,
   'Let Gwin be humbled,'
They cry, 'and let ten thousand lives
   'Pay for the tyrant's head.'

From tow'r to tow'r the watchmen cry,
   'O Gwin, the son of Nore,
'Arouse thyself! the nations black,
   'Like clouds, come rolling o'er!'

Gwin rear'd his shield, his palace shakes,
   His chiefs come rushing round;
Each, like an awful thunder cloud,
   With voice of solemn sound.

Like reared stones around a grave
   They stand around the King;
Then suddenly each seiz'd his spear,
   And clashing steel does ring.

The husbandman does leave his plow
  To wade thro' fields of gore;
The merchant binds his brows in steel,
  And leaves the trading shore;

The shepherd leaves his mellow pipe,
  And sounds the trumpet shrill;
The workman throws his hammer down
  To heave the bloody bill.

Like the tall ghost of Barraton,
  Who sports in stormy sky,
Gwin leads his host as black as night,
  When pestilence does fly.

With horses and with chariots –
  And all his spearmen bold,
March to the sound of mournful song,
  Like clouds around him roll'd.

Gwin lifts his hand – the nations halt;
  'Prepare for war,' he cries –
Gordred appears! – his frowning brow
  Troubles our northern skies.

The armies stand, like balances
  Held in th' Almighty's hand; –
'Gwin, thou hast fill'd thy measure up,
  'Thou'rt swept from out the land.'

And now the raging armies rush'd,
  Like warring mighty seas;
The Heav'ns are shook with roaring war,
  The dust ascends the skies!

Earth smokes with blood, and groans, and shakes,
  To drink her children's gore,
A sea of blood; nor can the eye
  See to the trembling shore!

And on the verge of this wild sea
   Famine and death doth cry;
The cries of women and of babes
   Over the field doth fly.

The King is seen raging afar,
   With all his men of might;
Like blazing comets, scattering death
   Thro' the red fev'rous night,

Beneath his arm like sheep they die,
   And groan upon the plain;
The battle faints, and bloody men
   Fight upon hills of slain.

Now death is sick, and riven men
   Labour and toil for life;
Steed rolls on steed, and shield on shield,
   Sunk in the sea of strife!

The god of war is drunk with blood,
   The earth doth faint and fail;
The stench of blood makes sick the heav'ns;
   Ghosts glut the throat of hell!

O what have Kings to answer for,
   Before that awful throne!
When thousand deaths for vengeance cry,
   And ghosts accusing groan!

Like blazing comets in the sky,
   That shake the stars of light,
Which drop like fruit unto the earth,
   Thro' the fierce burning night;

Like these did Gwin and Gordred meet,
   And the first blow decides;
Down from the brow unto the breast
   Gordred his head divides!

Gwin fell; the Sons of Norway fled,
　All that remain'd alive;
The rest did fill the vale of death,
　For them the eagles strive.

The river Dorman roll'd their blood
　Into the northern sea;
Who mourn'd his sons, and overwhelm'd
　The pleasant south country.

Minstrel's Song

From KING EDWARD THE THIRD

O Sons of Trojan Brutus, cloath'd in war,
Whose voices are the thunder of the field,
Rolling dark clouds o'er France, muffling the sun
In sickly darkness like a dim eclipse,
Threatening as the red brow of storms, as fire
Burning up nations in your wrath and fury!

Your ancestors came from the fires of Troy,
(Like lions rouz'd by light'ning from their dens,
Whose eyes do glare against the stormy fires)
Heated with war, fill'd with the blood of Greeks,
With helmets hewn, and shields covered with gore,
In navies black, broken with wind and tide!

They landed in firm array upon the rocks
Of Albion; they kiss'd the rocky shore;
'Be thou our mother, and our nurse,' they said;
'Our children's mother, and thou shalt be our grave;
'The sepulchre of ancient Troy, from whence
'Shall rise cities, and thrones, and arms, and awful pow'rs.'

Our fathers swarm from the ships. Giant voices
Are heard from the hills, the enormous sons
Of Ocean run from rocks and caves: wild men,
Naked and roaring like lions, hurling rocks,
And wielding knotty clubs, like oaks entangled
Thick as a forest, ready for the axe.

Our fathers move in firm array to battle,
The savage monsters rush like roaring fire;
Like as a forest roars, with crackling flames,
When the red lightning, borne by furious storms,
Lights on some woody shore; the parched heavens
Rain fire into the molten raging sea!

The smoking trees are strewn upon the shore,
Spoil'd of their verdure! O how oft have they
Defy'd the storm that howled o'er their heads!
Our fathers, sweating, lean on their spears, and view
The mighty dead: giant bodies streaming blood,
Dread visages, frowning in silent death!

Then Brutus spoke, inspir'd; our fathers sit
Attentive on the melancholy shore: –
Hear ye the voice of Brutus – 'The flowing waves
'Of time come rolling o'er my breast,' he said;
'And my heart labours with futurity:
'Our sons shall rule the empire of the sea.

'Their mighty wings shall stretch from east to west,
'Their nest is in the sea; but they shall roam
'Like eagles for the prey; nor shall the young
'Crave or be heard; for plenty shall bring forth,
'Cities shall sing, and vales in rich array
'Shall laugh, whose fruitful laps bend down with fulness.

'Our sons shall rise from thrones in joy,
'Each one buckling on his armour; Morning

'Shall be prevented by their swords gleaming,
'And Evening hear their song of victory!
'Their towers shall be built upon the rocks,
'Their daughters shall sing, surrounded with shining spears!

'Liberty shall stand upon the cliffs of Albion,
'Casting her blue eyes over the green ocean;
'Or, tow'ring, stand upon the roaring waves,
'Stretching her mighty spear o'er distant lands;
'While, with her eagle wings, she covereth
'Fair Albion's shore, and all her families.'

SONGS OF INNOCENCE

1789

Introduction

Piping down the valleys wild,
Piping songs of pleasant glee,
On a cloud I saw a child,
And he laughing said to me:

'Pipe a song about a Lamb!'
So I piped with merry chear.
'Piper, pipe that song again;'
So I piped: he wept to hear.

'Drop thy pipe, thy happy pipe,
'Sing thy songs of happy chear:'
So I sung the same again,
While he wept with joy to hear.

'Piper, sit thee down and write
'In a book that all may read.'
So he vanish'd from my sight,
And I pluck'd a hollow reed,

And I made a rural pen,
And I stain'd the water clear,
And I wrote my happy songs
Every child may joy to hear.

The Shepherd

How sweet is the Shepherd's sweet lot!
From the morn to the evening he strays;
He shall follow his sheep all the day,
And his tongue shall be filled with praise.

For he hears the lamb's innocent call,
And he hears the ewe's tender reply;
He is watchful while they are in peace,
For they know when their Shepherd is nigh.

The Ecchoing Green

The Sun does arise,
And make happy the skies;
The merry bells ring
To welcome the Spring;
The skylark and thrush,
The birds of the bush,
Sing louder around
To the bells' chearful sound,
While our sports shall be seen
On the Ecchoing Green.

Old John, with white hair,
Does laugh away care,
Sitting under the oak,
Among the old folk.
They laugh at our play,
And soon they all say:
'Such, such were the joys
'When we all, girls & boys,
'In our youth time were seen
'On the Ecchoing Green.'

Till the little ones, weary,
No more can be merry;
The sun does descend,
And our sports have an end.
Round the laps of their mothers

Many sisters and brothers,
Like birds in their nest,
Are ready for rest,
And sport no more seen
On the darkening Green.

The Lamb

Little Lamb, who made thee?
Dost thou know who made thee?
Gave thee life, & bid thee feed
By the stream & o'er the mead;
Gave thee clothing of delight,
Softest clothing, wooly, bright;
Gave thee such a tender voice,
Making all the vales rejoice?
Little Lamb, who made thee?
Dost thou know who made thee?

Little Lamb, I'll tell thee,
Little Lamb, I'll tell thee:
He is called by thy name,
For he calls himself a Lamb.
He is meek, & he is mild;
He became a little child.
I, a child, & thou a lamb,
We are called by his name.
Little Lamb, God bless thee!
Little Lamb, God bless thee!

The Little Black Boy

My mother bore me in the southern wild,
And I am black, but O! my soul is white;
White as an angel is the English child,
But I am black, as if bereav'd of light.

My mother taught me underneath a tree,
And sitting down before the heat of day,
She took me on her lap and kissed me,
And pointing to the east, began to say:

'Look on the rising sun: there God does live,
'And gives his light, and gives his heat away;
'And flowers and trees and beasts and men receive
'Comfort in morning, joy in the noonday.

'And we are put on earth a little space,
'That we may learn to bear the beams of love;
'And these black bodies and this sunburnt face
'Is but a cloud, and like a shady grove.

'For when our souls have learn'd the heat to bear,
'The cloud will vanish; we shall hear his voice,
'Saying: "Come out from the grove, my love & care,
'"And round my golden tent like lambs rejoice".'

Thus did my mother say, and kissed me;
And thus I say to little English boy:
When I from black and he from white cloud free,
And round the tent of God like lambs we joy,

I'll shade him from the heat, till he can bear
To lean in joy upon our father's knee;
And then I'll stand and stroke his silver hair,
And be like him, and he will then love me.

The Blossom

Merry, Merry Sparrow!
Under leaves so green
A happy Blossom

Sees you swift as arrow
Seek your cradle narrow
Near my Bosom.

Pretty, Pretty Robin!
Under leaves so green
A happy Blossom
Hears you sobbing, sobbing,
Pretty, Pretty Robin,
Near my Bosom.

The Chimney Sweeper

When my mother died I was very young,
And my father sold me while yet my tongue
Could scarcely cry ''weep! 'weep! 'weep! 'weep!''
So your chimneys I sweep, & in soot I sleep.

There's little Tom Dacre, who cried when his head,
That curl'd like a lamb's back, was shav'd: so I said
'Hush, Tom! never mind it, for when your head's bare
'You know that the soot cannot spoil your white hair.'

And so he was quiet, & that very night,
As Tom was a-sleeping, he had such a sight!
That thousands of sweepers, Dick, Joe, Ned, & Jack,
Were all of them lock'd up in coffins of black.

And by came an Angel who had a bright key,
And he open'd the coffins & set them all free;
Then down a green plain leaping, laughing, they run,
And wash in a river, and shine in the Sun.

Then naked & white, all their bags left behind,
They rise upon clouds and sport in the wind;
And the Angel told Tom, if he'd be a good boy,
He'd have God for his father, & never want joy.

And so Tom awoke; and we rose in the dark,
And got with our bags & our brushes to work.
Tho' the morning was cold, Tom was happy & warm;
So if all do their duty they need not fear harm.

The Little Boy Lost

'Father! father! where are you going?
'O do not walk so fast.
'Speak, father, speak to your little boy,
'Or else I shall be lost.'

The night was dark, no father was there;
The child was wet with dew;
The mire was deep, & the child did weep,
And away the vapour flew.

The Little Boy Found

The little boy lost in the lonely fen,
Led by the wand'ring light,
Began to cry; but God, ever nigh,
Appear'd like his father in white.

He kissed the child & by the hand led
And to his mother brought,
Who in sorrow pale, thro' the lonely dale,
Her little boy weeping sought.

Laughing Song

When the green woods laugh with the voice of joy,
And the dimpling stream runs laughing by;
When the air does laugh with our merry wit,
And the green hill laughs with the noise of it;

When the meadows laugh with lively green,
And the grasshopper laughs in the merry scene,
When Mary and Susan and Emily
With their sweet round mouths sing 'Ha, Ha, He!'

When the painted birds laugh in the shade,
Where our table with cherries and nuts is spread,
Come live & be merry, and join with me,
To sing the sweet chorus of 'Ha, Ha, He!'

A Cradle Song

Sweet dreams, form a shade
O'er my lovely infant's head;
Sweet dreams of pleasant streams
By happy, silent, moony beams.

Sweet sleep, with soft down
Weave thy brows an infant crown
Sweet sleep, Angel mild,
Hover o'er my happy child.

Sweet smiles, in the night
Hover over my delight;
Sweet smiles, Mother's smiles,
All the livelong night beguiles.

Sweet moans, dovelike sighs,
Chase not slumber from thy eyes.
Sweet moans, sweeter smiles,
All the dovelike moans beguiles.

Sleep, sleep, happy child,
All creation slept and smil'd;
Sleep, sleep, happy sleep,
While o'er thee thy mother weep.

Sweet babe, in thy face
Holy image I can trace.
Sweet babe, once like thee,
Thy maker lay and wept for me,

Wept for me, for thee, for all,
When he was an infant small.
Thou his image ever see,
Heavenly face that smiles on thee,

Smiles on thee, on me, on all;
Who became an infant small.
Infant smiles are his own smiles;
Heaven & earth to peace beguiles.

The Divine Image

To Mercy, Pity, Peace, and Love
All pray in their distress;
And to these virtues of delight
Return their thankfulness.

For Mercy, Pity, Peace, and Love
Is God, our father dear,
And Mercy, Pity, Peace, and Love
Is Man, his child and care.

For Mercy has a human heart,
Pity a human face,
And Love, the human form divine,
And Peace, the human dress.

Then every man, of every clime,
That prays in his distress,
Prays to the human form divine,
Love, Mercy, Pity, Peace.

And all must love the human form,
In heathen, turk, or jew;
Where Mercy, Love, & Pity dwell
There God is dwelling too.

Holy Thursday

'Twas on a Holy Thursday, their innocent faces clean,
The children walking two & two, in red & blue & green,
Grey-headed beadles walk'd before, with wands as white as
    snow,
Till into the high dome of Paul's they like Thames' waters
    flow.

O what a multitude they seem'd, these flowers of London
    town!
Seated in companies they sit with radiance all their own.
The hum of multitudes was there, but multitudes of lambs,
Thousands of little boys & girls raising their innocent hands.

Now like a mighty wind they raise to heaven the voice of
    song,
Or like harmonious thunderings the seats of heaven among.
Beneath them sit the aged men, wise guardians of the poor;
Then cherish pity, lest you drive an angel from your door.

Night

The sun descending in the west,
The evening star does shine;
The birds are silent in their nest,
And I must seek for mine.

The moon like a flower
In heaven's high bower,
With silent delight
Sits and smiles on the night.

Farewell, green fields and happy groves,
Where flocks have took delight.
Where lambs have nibbled, silent moves
The feet of angels bright;
Unseen they pour blessing
And joy without ceasing,
On each bud and blossom,
And each sleeping bosom.

They look in every thoughtless nest,
Where birds are cover'd warm;
They visit caves of every beast,
To keep them all from harm.
If they see any weeping
That should have been sleeping,
They pour sleep on their head,
And sit down by their bed.

When wolves and tygers howl for prey,
They pitying stand and weep;
Seeking to drive their thirst away,
And keep them from the sheep;
But if they rush dreadful,
The angels, most heedful,
Receive each mild spirit,
New worlds to inherit.

And there the lion's ruddy eyes
Shall flow with tears of gold,
And pitying the tender cries,
And walking round the fold,

Saying 'Wrath, by his meekness,
'And by his health, sickness
'Is driven away
'From our immortal day.

'And now beside thee, bleating lamb,
'I can lie down and sleep;
'Or think on him who bore thy name,
'Graze after thee and weep.
'For, wash'd in life's river,
'My bright mane for ever
'Shall shine like the gold
'As I guard o'er the fold.'

Spring

Sound the Flute!
Now it's mute.
Birds delight
Day and Night;
Nightingale
In the dale,
Lark in Sky,
Merrily,
Merrily, Merrily, to welcome in the Year.

Little Boy,
Full of joy;
Little Girl,
Sweet and small;
Cock does crow,
So do you;
Merry voice,
Infant noise,
Merrily, Merrily, to welcome in the Year.

Little Lamb,
Here I am;
Come and lick
My white neck;
Let me pull
Your soft Wool;
Let me kiss
Your soft face:
Merrily, Merrily, we welcome in the Year.

Nurse's Song

When the voices of children are heard on the green
And laughing is heard on the hill,
My heart is at rest within my breast
And everything else is still.

'Then come home, my children, the sun is gone down
'And the dews of night arise;
'Come, come, leave off play, and let us away
'Till the morning appears in the skies.'

'No, no, let us play, for it is yet day
'And we cannot go to sleep;
'Besides, in the sky the little birds fly
'And the hills are all cover'd with sheep.'

'Well, well, go & play till the light fades away
'And then go home to bed.'
The little ones leaped & shouted & laugh'd
And all the hills ecchoed.

Infant Joy

'I have no name:
'I am but two days old.'
What shall I call thee?

'I happy am,
'Joy is my name.'
Sweet joy befall thee!

Pretty joy!
Sweet joy but two days old,
Sweet joy I call thee:
Thou dost smile,
I sing the while,
Sweet joy befall thee!

A Dream

Once a dream did weave a shade
O'er my Angel-guarded bed,
That an Emmet lost its way
Where on grass methought I lay.

Troubled, 'wilder'd, and forlorn,
Dark, benighted, travel-worn,
Over many a tangled spray,
All heart-broke I heard her say:

'O, my children! do they cry?
'Do they hear their father sigh?
'Now they look abroad to see:
'Now return and weep for me.'

Pitying, I drop'd a tear;
But I saw a glow-worm near,
Who replied: 'What wailing wight
'Calls the watchman of the night?

'I am set to light the ground,
'While the beetle goes his round:
'Follow now the beetle's hum;
'Little wanderer, hie thee home.'

On Another's Sorrow

Can I see another's woe,
And not be in sorrow too?
Can I see another's grief,
And not seek for kind relief?

Can I see a falling tear,
And not feel my sorrow's share?
Can a father see his child
Weep, nor be with sorrow fill'd?

Can a mother sit and hear
An infant groan an infant fear?
No, no! never can it be!
Never, never can it be!

And can he who smiles on all
Hear the wren with sorrows small,
Hear the small bird's grief & care,
Hear the woes that infants bear,

And not sit beside the nest,
Pouring pity in their breast;
And not sit the cradle near,
Weeping tear on infant's tear;

And not sit both night & day,
Wiping all our tears away?
O, no! never can it be!
Never, never can it be!

He doth give his joy to all;
He becomes an infant small;
He becomes a man of woe;
He doth feel the sorrow too.

Think not thou canst sigh a sigh
And thy maker is not by;
Think not thou canst weep a tear
And thy maker is not near.

O! he gives to us his joy
That our grief he may destroy;
Till our grief is fled & gone
He doth sit by us and moan.

SONGS OF EXPERIENCE

1794

Introduction

Hear the voice of the Bard!
Who Present, Past, & Future, sees;
Whose ears have heard
The Holy Word
That walk'd among the ancient trees,

Calling the lapsed Soul,
And weeping in the evening dew;
That might controll
The starry pole,
And fallen, fallen light renew!

'O Earth, O Earth, return!
'Arise from out the dewy grass;
'Night is worn,
'And the morn
'Rises from the slumberous mass.

'Turn away no more;
'Why wilt thou turn away?
'The starry floor,
'The wat'ry shore,
'Is giv'n thee till the break of day.'

Earth's Answer

Earth rais'd up her head
From the darkness dread & drear.
Her light fled,
Stony dread!
And her locks cover'd with grey despair.

'Prison'd on wat'ry shore,
'Starry Jealousy does keep my den
'Cold and hoar,
'Weeping o'er,
'I hear the Father of the ancient men.

'Selfish father of men!
'Cruel, jealous, selfish fear!
'Can delight,
'Chain'd in night,
'The virgins of youth and morning bear?

'Does spring hide its joy
'When buds and blossoms grow?
'Does the sower
'Sow by night,
'Or the plowman in darkness plow?

'Break this heavy chain
'That does freeze my bones around.
'Selfish! vain!
'Eternal bane!
'That free Love with bondage bound.'

The Clod & the Pebble

'Love seeketh not Itself to please,
'Nor for itself hath any care,
'But for another gives its ease,
'And builds a Heaven in Hell's despair.'

So sung a little Clod of Clay
Trodden with the cattle's feet,
But a Pebble of the brook
Warbled out these metres meet:

'Love seeketh only Self to please,
'To bind another to Its delight,
'Joys in another's loss of ease,
'And builds a Hell in Heaven's despite.

Holy Thursday

Is this a holy thing to see
In a rich and fruitful land,
Babes reduc'd to misery,
Fed with cold and usurous hand?

Is that trembling cry a song?
Can it be a song of joy?
And so many children poor?
It is a land of poverty!

And their sun does never shine,
And their fields are black & bare,
And their ways are fill'd with thorns:
It is eternal winter there.

For where-e'er the sun does shine,
And where-e'er the rain does fall,
Babe can never hunger there,
Nor poverty the mind appall.

The Little Girl Lost

In futurity
I prophetic see
That the earth from sleep
(Grave the sentence deep)

Shall arise and seek
For her maker meek;

43

And the desart wild
Become a garden mild.

*

In the southern clime
Where the summer's prime
Never fades away,
Lovely Lyca lay.

Seven summers old
Lovely Lyca told;
She had wander'd long
Hearing wild birds' song.

'Sweet sleep, come to me
'Underneath this tree.
'Do father, mother weep,
'Where can Lyca sleep?

'Lost in desart wild
'Is your little child.
'How can Lyca sleep
'If her mother weep?

'If her heart does ake
'Then let Lyca wake;
'If my mother sleep,
'Lyca shall not weep.

'Frowning, frowning night,
'O'er this desart bright
'Let thy moon arise
'While I close my eyes.'

Sleeping Lyca lay
While the beasts of prey,
Come from caverns deep,
View'd the maid asleep.

The kingly lion stood
And the virgin view'd,
Then he gamboll'd round
O'er the hallow'd ground.

Leopards, tygers, play
Round her as she lay,
While the lion old
Bow'd his mane of gold

And her bosom lick,
And upon her neck
From his eyes of flame
Ruby tears there came;

While the lioness
Loos'd her slender dress,
And naked they convey'd
To caves the sleeping maid.

The Little Girl Found

All the night in woe
Lyca's parents go
Over vallies deep,
While the desarts weep.

Tired and woe-begone,
Hoarse with making moan,
Arm in arm seven days
They trac'd the desert ways.

Seven nights they sleep
Among shadows deep,
And dream they see their child
Starv'd in desert wild.

Pale, thro' pathless ways
The fancied image strays
Famish'd, weeping, weak,
With hollow piteous shriek.

Rising from unrest,
The trembling woman prest
With feet of weary woe:
She could no further go.

In his arms he bore
Her, arm'd with sorrow sore,
Till before their way
A couching lion lay.

Turning back was vain:
Soon his heavy mane
Bore them to the ground.
Then he stalk'd around,

Smelling to his prey;
But their fears allay
When he licks their hands,
And silent by them stands.

They look upon his eyes
Fill'd with deep surprise,
And wondering behold
A spirit arm'd in gold.

On his head a crown,
On his shoulders down
Flow'd his golden hair.
Gone was all their care.

'Follow me,' he said;
'Weep not for the maid;
'In my palace deep
'Lyca lies asleep.'

Then they followed
Where the vision led,
And saw their sleeping child
Among tygers wild.

To this day they dwell
In a lonely dell;
Nor fear the wolvish howl
Nor the lions' growl.

The Chimney Sweeper

A little black thing among the snow,
Crying ''weep! 'weep!' in notes of woe!
'Where are thy father & mother? say?'
'They are both gone up to the church to pray.

'Because I was happy upon the heath,
'And smil'd among the winter's snow,
'They cloth'd me in the clothes of death,
'And taught me to sing the notes of woe.

'And because I am happy & dance & sing,
'They think they have done me no injury,
'And are gone to praise God & his Priest & King,
'Who make up a heaven of our misery.'

Nurse's Song

When the voices of children are heard on the green
And whisp'rings are in the dale,
The days of my youth rise fresh in my mind,
My face turns green and pale.

Then come home, my children, the sun is gone down,
And the dews of night arise;
Your spring & your day are wasted in play,
And your winter and night in disguise.

The Sick Rose

O Rose, thou art sick!
The invisible worm
That flies in the night,
In the howling storm,

Has found out thy bed
Of crimson joy:
And his dark secret love
Does thy life destroy.

The Fly

Little Fly,
Thy summer's play
My thoughtless hand
Has brush'd away.

Am not I
A fly like thee?
Or art not thou
A man like me?

For I dance,
And drink, & sing,
Till some blind hand
Shall brush my wing.

If thought is life
And strength & breath,
And the want
Of thought is death;

Then am I
A happy fly,
If I live
Or if I die.

The Angel

I Dreamt a Dream! what can it mean?
And that I was a maiden Queen,
Guarded by an Angel mild:
Witless woe was ne'er beguil'd!

And I wept both night and day,
And he wip'd my tears away,
And I wept both day and night,
And hid from him my heart's delight.

So he took his wings and fled;
Then the morn blush'd rosy red;
I dried my tears, & arm'd my fears
With ten thousand shields and spears.

Soon my Angel came again:
I was arm'd, he came in vain;
For the time of youth was fled,
And grey hairs were on my head.

The Tyger

Tyger! Tyger! burning bright
In the forests of the night,
What immortal hand or eye
Could frame thy fearful symmetry?

In what distant deeps or skies
Burnt the fire of thine eyes?
On what wings dare he aspire?
What the hand dare sieze the fire?

And what shoulder, & what art,
Could twist the sinews of thy heart?
And when thy heart began to beat,
What dread hand? & what dread feet?

What the hammer? what the chain?
In what furnace was thy brain?
What the anvil? what dread grasp
Dare its deadly terrors clasp?

When the stars threw down their spears,
And water'd heaven with their tears,
Did he smile his work to see?
Did he who made the Lamb make thee?

Tyger! Tyger! burning bright
In the forests of the night,
What immortal hand or eye
Dare frame thy fearful symmetry?

My Pretty Rose Tree

A flower was offer'd to me,
Such a flower as May never bore;
But I said 'I've a Pretty Rose-tree,'
And I passed the sweet flower o'er.

Then I went to my Pretty Rose-tree,
To tend her by day and by night;
But my Rose turn'd away with jealousy,
And her thorns were my only delight.

Ah! Sun-flower

Ah, Sun-flower! weary of time,
Who countest the steps of the Sun,
Seeking after that sweet golden clime
Where the traveller's journey is done:

Where the Youth pined away with desire,
And the pale Virgin shrouded in snow
Arise from their graves, and aspire
Where my Sun-flower wishes to go.

The Lilly

The modest Rose puts forth a thorn,
The humble Sheep a threat'ning horn;
While the Lilly white shall in Love delight,
Nor a thorn, nor a threat, stain her beauty bright.

The Garden of Love

I went to the Garden of Love,
And saw what I never had seen:
A Chapel was built in the midst,
Where I used to play on the green.

And the gates of this Chapel were shut,
And 'Thou shalt not' writ over the door;
So I turn'd to the Garden of Love
That so many sweet flowers bore;

And I saw it was filled with graves,
And tomb-stones where flowers should be;
And Priests in black gowns were walking their rounds,
And binding with briars my joys & desires.

The Little Vagabond

Dear Mother, dear Mother, the Church is cold,
But the Ale-house is healthy & pleasant & warm;
Besides I can tell where I am used well,
Such usage in heaven will never do well.

But if at the Church they would give us some Ale,
And a pleasant fire our souls to regale,
We'd sing and we'd pray all the live-long day,
Nor ever once wish from the Church to stray.

Then the Parson might preach, & drink, & sing,
And we'd be as happy as birds in the spring;
And modest dame Lurch, who is always at Church,
Would not have bandy children, nor fasting, nor birch.

And God, like a father rejoicing to see
His children as pleasant and happy as he,
Would have no more quarrel with the Devil or the Barrel,
But kiss him, & give him both drink and apparel.

London

I wander thro' each charter'd street,
Near where the charter'd Thames does flow,
And mark in every face I meet
Marks of weakness, marks of woe.

In every cry of every Man,
In every Infant's cry of fear,
In every voice, in every ban,
The mind-forg'd manacles I hear.

How the Chimney-sweeper's cry
Every black'ning Church appalls;
And the hapless Soldier's sigh
Runs in blood down Palace walls.

But most thro' midnight streets I hear
How the youthful Harlot's curse
Blasts the new born Infant's tear,
And blights with plagues the Marriage hearse.

The Human Abstract

Pity would be no more
If we did not make somebody Poor;
And Mercy no more could be
If all were as happy as we.

And mutual fear brings peace,
Till the selfish loves increase:
Then Cruelty knits a snare,
And spreads his baits with care.

He sits down with holy fears,
And waters the ground with tears;
Then Humility takes its root
Underneath his foot.

Soon spreads the dismal shade
Of Mystery over his head;
And the Catterpiller and Fly
Feed on the Mystery.

And it bears the fruit of Deceit,
Ruddy and sweet to eat;
And the Raven his nest has made
In its thickest shade.

The Gods of the earth and sea
Sought thro' Nature to find this Tree;
But their search was all in vain:
There grows one in the Human Brain.

Infant Sorrow

My mother groan'd! my father wept.
Into the dangerous world I leapt:
Helpless, naked, piping loud:
Like a fiend hid in a cloud.

Struggling in my father's hands,
Striving against my swadling bands.
Bound and weary I thought best
To sulk upon my mother's breast.

A Poison Tree

I was angry with my friend:
I told my wrath, my wrath did end.
I was angry with my foe:
I told it not, my wrath did grow.

And I water'd it in fears,
Night & morning with my tears;
And I sunned it with smiles,
And with soft deceitful wiles.

And it grew both day and night,
Till it bore an apple bright;
And my foe beheld it shine,
And he knew that it was mine,

And into my garden stole
When the night had veil'd the pole:
In the morning glad I see
My foe outstretch'd beneath the tree.

A Little Boy Lost

'Nought loves another as itself,
'Nor venerates another so,
'Nor is it possible to Thought
'A greater than itself to know:

'And Father, how can I love you
'Or any of my brothers more?
'I love you like the little bird
'That picks up crumbs around the door.'

The Priest sat by and heard the child,
In trembling zeal he siez'd his hair:
He led him by his little coat,
And all admir'd the Priestly care.

And standing on the altar high,
'Lo! what a fiend is here!' said he,
'One who sets reason up for judge
'Of our most holy Mystery.'

The weeping child could not be heard,
The weeping parents wept in vain;
They strip'd him to his little shirt,
And bound him in an iron chain;

And burn'd him in a holy place,
Where many had been burn'd before:
The weeping parents wept in vain.
Are such things done on Albion's shore?

A Little Girl Lost

Children of the future Age
Reading this indignant page,
Know that in a former time
Love! sweet Love! was thought a crime.

In the Age of Gold,
Free from winter's cold,
Youth and maiden bright
To the holy light,
Naked in the sunny beams delight.

Once a youthful pair,
Fill'd with softest care,
Met in garden bright
Where the holy light
Had just remov'd the curtains of the night.

There, in rising day,
On the grass they play;
Parent were afar,
Strangers came not near,
And the maiden soon forgot her fear.

Tired with kisses sweet,
They agree to meet
When the silent sleep
Waves o'er heaven's deep,
And the weary tired wanderers weep.

To her father white
Came the maiden bright;
But his loving look,
Like the holy book,
All her tender limbs with terror shook.

'Ona! pale and weak!
'To thy father speak:
'O, the trembling fear!
'O, the dismal care!
'That shakes the blossoms of my hoary hair.'

To Tirzah

Probably added about 1801

Whate'er is Born of Mortal Birth
Must be consumed with the Earth
To rise from Generation free:
Then what have I to do with thee?

The Sexes sprung from Shame & Pride,
Blow'd in the morn; in evening died;
But Mercy chang'd Death into Sleep;
The Sexes rose to work & weep.

Thou, Mother of my Mortal part,
With cruelty didst mould my Heart,
And with false self-deceiving tears
Didst bind my Nostrils, Eyes, & Ears:

Didst close my Tongue in senseless clay,
And me to Mortal Life betray.
The Death of Jesus set me free:
Then what have I to do with thee?

The School Boy

I love to rise in a summer morn
When the birds sing on every tree;
The distant huntsman winds his horn,
And the sky-lark sings with me.
O! what sweet company.

But to go to school in a summer morn,
O! it drives all joy away;
Under a cruel eye outworn,
The little ones spend the day
In sighing and dismay.

Ah! then at times I drooping sit,
And spend many an anxious hour,
Nor in my book can I take delight,
Nor sit in learning's bower,
Worn thro' with the dreary shower.

How can the bird that is born for joy
Sit in a cage and sing?
How can a child, when fears annoy,
But droop his tender wing,
And forget his youthful spring?

O! father & mother, if buds are nip'd
And blossoms blown away,
And if the tender plants are strip'd
Of their joy in the springing day,
By sorrow and care's dismay,

How shall the summer arise in joy,
Or the summer fruits appear?
Or how shall we gather what griefs destroy,
Or bless the mellowing year,
When the blasts of winter appear?

The Voice of the Ancient Bard

Youth of delight, come hither,
And see the opening morn,
Image of truth new born.
Doubt is fled, & clouds of reason,

Dark disputes & artful teazing.
Folly is an endless maze,
Tangled roots perplex her ways.
How many have fallen there!
They stumble all night over bones of the dead,
And feel they know not what but care,
And wish to lead others, when they should be led.

A Divine Image

Cruelty has a Human Heart,
And Jealousy a Human Face;
Terror the Human Form Divine,
And Secrecy the Human Dress.

The Human Dress is forged Iron,
The Human Form a fiery Forge,
The Human Face a Furnace seal'd,
The Human Heart its hungry Gorge.

POEMS FROM MSS

Written about 1793

Never seek to tell thy love
Love that never told can be;
For the gentle wind does move
Silently, invisibly.

I told my love, I told my love,
I told her all my heart,
Trembling, cold, in ghastly fears –
Ah, she doth depart.

Soon as she was gone from me
A traveller came by
Silently, invisibly –
O, was no deny.

⌇

I laid me down upon a bank
Where love lay sleeping.
I heard among the rushes dank
Weeping, Weeping.

Then I went to the heath & the wild
To the thistles & thorns of the waste
And they told me how they were beguil'd,
Driven out, & compel'd to be chaste.

⌇

I asked a thief to steal me a peach:
He turned up his eyes.
I ask'd a lithe lady to lie her down:
Holy & meek she cries.

As soon as I went an angel came.
He wink'd at the thief
And smil'd at the dame,
And without one word spoke
Had a peach from the tree,
And 'twixt earnest & joke
Enjoy'd the Lady.

∽

I fear'd the fury of my wind
Would blight all blossoms fair & true;
And my sun it shin'd & shin'd
And my wind it never blew.

But a blossom fair or true
Was not found on any tree;
For all blossoms grew & grew
Fruitless, false, tho' fair to see.

Infant Sorrow

My mother groan'd, my father wept;
Into the dangerous world I leapt,
Helpless, naked, piping loud,
Like a fiend hid in a cloud.

Struggling in my father's hands
Striving against my swaddling bands,
Bound & weary, I thought best
To sulk upon my mother's breast.

When I saw that rage was vain,
And to sulk would nothing gain,
Turning many a trick & wile,
I began to soothe & smile.

And I sooth'd day after day
Till upon the ground I stray;
And I smil'd night after night,
Seeking only for delight.

And I saw before me shine
Clusters of the wand'ring vine,
And many a lovely flower & tree
Stretch'd their blossoms out to me.

My father then with holy look,
In his hands a holy book,
Pronounc'd curses on my head
And bound me in a mirtle shade.

In a Mirtle Shade

Why should I be bound to thee,
O my lovely mirtle tree?
Love, free love, cannot be bound
To any tree that grows on ground.

O, how sick & weary I
Underneath my mirtle lie,
Like to dung upon the ground
Underneath my mirtle bound.

Oft my mirtle sigh'd in vain
To behold my heavy chain;
Oft my father saw us sigh,
And laugh'd at our simplicity.

So I smote him & his gore
Stain'd the roots my mirtle bore.
But the time of youth is fled,
And grey hairs are on my head.

∽

Silent, Silent Night
Quench the holy light
Of thy torches bright.

For possess'd of Day
Thousand spirits stray
That sweet joys betray.

Why should joys be sweet
Used with deceit
Nor with sorrows meet?

But an honest joy
Does itself destroy
For a harlot coy.

ᔧ

Thou hast a lap full of seed,
And this is a fine country.
Why dost thou not cast thy seed
And live in it merrily?

Shall I cast it on the sand
And turn it into fruitful land?
For on no other ground
Can I sow my seed
Without tearing up
Some stinking weed.

Soft Snow

I walked abroad in a snowy day:
I ask'd the soft snow with me to play:
She play'd & she melted in all her prime,
And the winter call'd it a dreadful crime.

An Ancient Proverb

Remove away that black'ning church:
Remove away that marriage hearse:
Remove away that man of blood:
You'll quite remove the ancient curse.

To My Mirtle

To a lovely mirtle bound,
Blossoms show'ring all around,
O, how sick & weary I
Underneath my mirtle lie.
Why should I be bound to thee,
O, my lovely mirtle tree?

∽

Abstinence sows sand all over
The ruddy limbs & flaming hair,
But Desire Gratified
Plants fruits of life & beauty there.

∽

In a wife I would desire
What in whores is always found –
The lineaments of Gratified desire.

∽

'Let the Brothels of Paris be opened
'With many an alluring dance

'To awake the Pestilence thro' the city,'
Said the beautiful Queen of France.

The King awoke on his couch of gold,
As soon as he heard these tidings told:
'Arise & come, both fife & drum,
'And the Famine shall eat both crust & crumb.'

Then he swore a great & solemn Oath:
'To kill the people I am loth,
'But If they rebel, they must go to hell:
'They shall have a Priest & a passing bell.'

Then old Nobodaddy aloft
Farted & belch'd & cough'd,
And said, 'I love hanging & drawing & quartering
'Every bit as well as war & slaughtering.
'Damn praying & singing,
'Unless they will bring in
'The blood of ten thousand by fighting or swinging.'

The Queen of France just touched this Globe,
And the Pestilence darted from her robe;
But our good Queen quite grows to the ground,
And a great many suckers grow all round.

Fayette beside King Lewis stood;
He saw him sign his hand;
And he saw the famine rage
About the fruitful land.

Fayette beheld the Queen to smile
And wink her lovely eye;
And soon he saw the pestilence
From street to street to fly.

Fayette beheld the King & Queen
In tears & iron bound;
But mute Fayette wept tear for tear,
And guarded them around.

Fayette, Fayette, thou'rt bought & sold,
And sold is thy happy morrow;
Thou gavest the tears of Pity away
In exchange for the tears of sorrow.

Who will exchange his own fire side
For the steps of another's door?
Who will exchange his wheaten loaf
For the links of a dungeon floor?

O, who would smile on the wintry seas,
& Pity the stormy roar?
Or who will exchange his new born child
For the dog at the wintry door?

POEMS FROM MSS

Written about 1803

Mock on, Mock on Voltaire, Rousseau:
Mock on, Mock on: 'tis all in vain!
You throw the sand against the wind,
And the wind blows it back again.

And every sand becomes a Gem
Reflected in the beams divine;
Blown back they blind the mocking Eye,
But still in Israel's paths they shine.

The Atoms of Democritus
And Newton's Particles of light
Are sands upon the Red sea shore,
Where Israel's tents do shine so bright.

Auguries of Innocence

To see a World in a Grain of Sand
And a Heaven in a Wild Flower,
Hold Infinity in the palm of your hand
And Eternity in an hour.

A Robin Red breast in a Cage
Puts all Heaven in a Rage.
A dove house fill'd with doves & Pigeons
Shudders Hell thro' all its regions.
A dog starv'd at his Master's Gate
Predicts the ruin of the State.
A Horse misus'd upon the Road
Calls to Heaven for Human blood.
Each outcry of the hunted Hare

A fibre from the Brain does tear.
A Skylark wounded in the wing,
A Cherubim does cease to sing.
The Game Cock clip'd & arm'd for fight
Does the Rising Sun affright.
Every Wolf's & Lion's howl
Raises from Hell a Human Soul.
The wild deer, wand'ring here & there,
Keeps the Human Soul from Care.
The Lamb misus'd breeds Public strife
And yet forgives the Butcher's Knife.
The Bat that flits at close of Eve
Has left the Brain that won't Believe.
The Owl that calls upon the Night
Speaks the Unbeliever's fright.
He who shall hurt the little Wren
Shall never be belov'd by Men.
He who the Ox to wrath has mov'd
Shall never be by Woman lov'd.
The wanton Boy that kills the Fly
Shall feel the Spider's enmity.
He who torments the Chafer's sprite
Weaves a Bower in endless Night.
The Catterpiller on the Leaf
Repeats to thee thy Mother's grief.
Kill not the Moth nor Butterfly,
For the Last Judgment draweth nigh.
He who shall train the Horse to War
Shall never pass the Polar Bar.
The Begger's Dog & Widow's Cat,
Feed them & thou wilt grow fat.
The Gnat that sings his Summer's song
Poison gets from Slander's tongue.
The poison of the Snake & Newt
Is the sweat of Envy's Foot.

The Poison of the Honey Bee
Is the Artist's Jealousy.
The Prince's Robes & Beggar's Rags
Are Toadstools on the Miser's Bags.
A truth that's told with bad intent
Beats all the Lies you can invent.
It is right it should be so;
Man was made for Joy & Woe;
And when this we rightly know
Thro' the World we safely go.
Joy & Woe are woven fine,
A Clothing for the Soul divine;
Under every grief & pine
Runs a joy with silken twine.
The Babe is more than swadling Bands;
Throughout all these Human Lands
Tools were made, & Born were hands,
Every Farmer Understands.
Every Tear in Every Eye
Becomes a Babe in Eternity;
This is caught by Females bright
And return'd to its own delight.
The Bleat, the Bark, Bellow & Roar
Are Waves that Beat on Heaven's Shore,
The Babe that weeps the Rod beneath
Writes Revenge in realms of death.
The Beggar's Rags, fluttering in Air,
Does to Rags the Heavens tear.
The Soldier, arm'd with Sword & Gun,
Palsied strikes the Summer's Sun.
The poor Man's Farthing is worth more
Than all the Gold on Afric's Shore.
One Mite wrung from the Labrer's hands
Shall buy & sell the Miser's Lands:
Or, if protected from on high,

Does that whole Nation sell & buy.
He who mocks the Infant's Faith
Shall be mock'd in Age & Death.
He who shall teach the Child to Doubt
The rotting Grave shall ne'er get out.
He who respects the Infant's faith
Triumphs over Hell & Death.
The Child's Toys & the Old Man's Reasons
Are the Fruits of the Two seasons.
The Questioner, who sits so sly,
Shall never know how to Reply.
He who replies to words of Doubt
Doth put the Light of Knowledge out.
The Strongest Poison ever known
Came from Caesar's Laurel Crown.
Nought can deform the Human Race
Like to the Armour's iron brace.
When Gold & Gems adorn the Plow
To peaceful Arts shall Envy Bow.
A Riddle or the Cricket's Cry
Is to Doubt a fit Reply.
The Emmet's Inch & Eagle's Mile
Make Lame Philosophy to smile.
He who Doubts from what he sees
Will ne'er Believe, do what you Please.
If the Sun & Moon should doubt,
They'd immediately Go out.
To be in a Passion you Good may do,
But no Good if a Passion is in you.
The Whore & Gambler, by the State
Licenc'd, build that Nation's Fate.
The Harlot's cry from Street to Street
Shall weave Old England's winding Sheet.
The Winner's Shout, the Loser's Curse,
Dance before dead England's Hearse.

Every Night & every Morn
Some to Misery are Born.
Every Morn & every Night
Some are Born to sweet delight.
Some are Born to sweet delight,
Some are Born to Endless Night.
We are led to Believe a Lie
When we see not Thro' the Eye
Which was Born in a Night to perish in a Night
When the Soul Slept in Beams of Light.
God Appears & God is Light
To those poor Souls who dwell in Night.
But does a Human Form Display
To those who Dwell in Realms of day.

POEM FROM MS

Written about 1810

I rose up at the dawn of day –
Get thee away! get thee away!
Pray'st thou for Riches? away! away!
This is the Throne of Mammon grey.

Said I, 'this sure is very odd.
'I took it to be the Throne of God.
'For every Thing besides I have:
'It is only for Riches that I can crave.

'I have Mental Joy & Mental Health
'And Mental Friends & Mental wealth;
'I've a Wife I love & that loves me;
'I've all but Riches Bodily.

'I am in God's presence night & day,
'And he never turns his face away.
'The accuser of sins by my side does stand
'And he holds my money bag in his hand.

'For my worldly things God makes him pay,
'And he'd pay more if to him I would pray;
'And so you may do the worst you can do:
'Be assur'd Mr devil I won't pray to you.

'Then If for Riches I must not Pray,
'God knows I little of Prayers need say.
'So as a Church is known by its Steeple,
'If I pray it must be for other People.

'He says, if I do not worship him for a God,
'I shall eat coarser food & go worse shod;
'So as I don't value such things as these,
'You must do, Mr devil, just as God please.'

THE EVERLASTING GOSPEL

Several Drafts

Written about 1818

There is not one Moral Virtue that Jesus Inculcated
but Plato & Cicero did Inculcate before him; what then
did Christ Inculcate? Forgiveness of Sins. This alone is
the Gospel, & this is the Life & Immortality brought to
light by Jesus, Even the Covenant of Jehovah, which is
This: If you forgive one another your Trespasses, so
shall Jehovah forgive you, That he himself may dwell
among you; but if you Avenge, you Murder the Divine
Image, & he cannot dwell among you; because you
Murder him he arises again, & you deny that he is
Arisen, & are blind to Spirit.

*

If Moral Virtue was Christianity,
Christ's Pretensions were all Vanity,
And Cai(a)phas & Pilate, Men
Praise Worthy, & the Lion's Den
And not the Sheepfold, Allegories
Of God & Heaven & their Glories.
The Moral Christian is the Cause
Of the Unbeliever & his Laws.
The Roman Virtues, Warlike Fame,
Take Jesus' & Jehovah's Name;
For what is Antichrist but those
Who against Sinners Heaven close
With Iron bars, in Virtuous State,
And Rhadamanthus at the Gate?

*

What can this Gospel of Jesus be?
What Life & Immortality,
What was it that he brought to Light
That Plato & Cicero did not write?
The Heathen Deities wrote them all,
These Moral Virtues, great & small.
What is the Accusation of Sin
But Moral Virtues' deadly Gin?
The Moral Virtues in their Pride
Did o'er the World triumphant ride
In Wars & Sacrifice for Sin,
And Souls to Hell ran trooping in.
The Accuser, Holy God of All
This Pharisaic Worldly Ball,
Amidst them in his Glory Beams
Upon the Rivers & the Streams.
Then Jesus rose & said to Me,
'Thy Sins are all forgiven thee.'
Loud Pilate Howl'd, loud Cai(a)phas yell'd,
When they the Gospel Light beheld.
It was when Jesus said to Me,
'Thy Sins are all forgiven thee.'
The Christian trumpets loud proclaim
Thro' all the World in Jesus' name
Mutual forgiveness of each Vice,
And oped the Gates of Paradise.
The Moral Virtues in Great fear
Formed the Cross & Nails & Spear,
And the Accuser standing by
Cried out, 'Crucify! Crucify!
'Our Moral Virtues ne'er can be,
'Nor Warlike pomp & Majesty;
'For Moral Virtues all begin
'In the Accusations of Sin,
'And all the Heroic Virtues End

'In destroying the Sinners' Friend.
'Am I not Lucifer the Great,
'And you my daughters in Great State,
'The fruit of my Mysterious Tree
'Of Good & Evil & Misery
'And Death & Hell, which now begin
'On everyone who Forgives Sin?'

*

The Vision of Christ that thou dost see
Is my Vision's Greatest Enemy:
Thine has a great hook nose like thine,
Mine has a snub nose like to mine:
Thine is the friend of All Mankind,
Mine speaks in parables to the Blind:
Thine loves the same world that mine hates,
Thy Heaven doors are my Hell Gates.
Socrates taught what Meletus
Loath'd as a Nation's Bitterest Curse,
And Cai(a)phas was in his own Mind
A benefactor to Mankind:
Both read the Bible day & night,
But thou read'st black where I read white.

*

Was Jesus gentle, or did he
Give any marks of Gentility?
When twelve years old he ran away
And left his Parents in dismay.
When after three days' sorrow found,
Loud as Sinai's trumpet sound:
'No Earthly Parents I confess –
'My Heavenly Father's business!

'Ye understand not what I say,
'And, angry, force me to obey.'
Obedience is a duty then,
And favour gains with God & Men.
John from the Wilderness loud cried;
Satan gloried in his Pride.
'Come,' said Satan, 'come away,
'I'll soon see if you'll obey!
'John for disobedience bled,
'But you can turn the stones to bread.
'God's high king & God's high Priest
'Shall Plant their Glories in your breast
'If Caiaphas you will obey,
'If Herod you with bloody Prey
'Feed with the sacrifice, & be
'Obedient, fall down, worship me.'
Thunders & lightnings broke around,
And Jesus' voice in thunders' sound:
'Thus I sieze the Spiritual Prey.
'Ye smiters with disease, make way.
'I come your King & God to sieze.
'Is God a smiter with disease?'
The God of this World raged in vain:
He bound Old Satan in his Chain,
And bursting forth, his furious ire
Became a Chariot of fire.
Throughout the land he took his course,
And traced diseases to their source:
He curs'd the Scribe & Pharisee,
Trampling down Hipocrisy:
Where'er his Chariot took its way,
There Gates of death let in the day,
Broke down from every Chain & Bar;
And Satan in his Spiritual War
Drag'd at his Chariot wheels: loud howl'd

The God of this World: louder roll'd
The Chariot Wheels, & louder still
His voice was heard from Zion's hill,
And in his hand the Scourge shone bright,
He scourg'd the Merchant Canaanite
From out the Temple of his Mind,
And in his Body tight does bind
Satan & all his Hellish Crew;
And thus with wrath he did subdue
The Serpent Bulk of Nature's dross,
Till He had nail'd it to the Cross.
He took on Sin in the Virgin's Womb,
And put it off on the Cross & Tomb
To be Worship'd by the Church of Rome.

*

Was Jesus Humble? or did he
Give any proofs of Humility?
When but a Child he ran away
And left his Parents in dismay.
When they had wonder'd three days long
These were the words upon his Tongue:
'No earthly Parents I confess:
'I am doing my Father's business.'
When the rich learned Pharisee
Came to consult him secretly,
Upon his heart with Iron pen
He wrote, 'Ye must be born again.'
He was too Proud to take a bribe;
He spoke with authority, not like a Scribe.
He says with most consummate Art,
'Follow me, I am meek & lowly of heart,'
As that is the only way to Escape
The Miser's net & the Glutton's trap.

He who loves his Enemies, hates his Friends;
This is surely not what Jesus intends;
He must mean the meer love of Civility,
And so he must mean concerning Humility;
But he acts with triumphant, honest pride,
And this is the Reason Jesus died.
If he had been Antichrist, Creeping Jesus,
He'd have done anything to please us:
Gone sneaking into the Synagogues
And not used the Elders & Priests like Dogs,
But humble as a Lamb or an Ass,
Obey himself to Caiaphas.
God wants not Man to humble himself:
This is the Trick of the Ancient Elf.
Humble toward God, Haughty toward Man,
This is the Race that Jesus ran,
And when he humbled himself to God,
Then descended the cruel rod.
'If thou humblest thyself, thou humblest me;
'Thou also dwelst in Eternity.
'Thou art a Man, God is no more,
'Thine own Humanity learn to Adore
'And thy Revenge Abroad display
'In terrors at the Last Judgment day.
'God's Mercy & Long Suffering
'Are but the Sinner to Judgment to bring.
'Thou on the Cross for them shalt pray
'And take Revenge at the last Day.
'Do what you will, this Life's a Fiction
'And is made up of Contradiction.'

*

Was Jesus Humble? or did he
Give any Proofs of Humility?

Boast of high Things with Humble tone,
And give with Charity a Stone?
When but a Child he ran away
And left his Parents in dismay.
When they had wander'd three days long
These were the words upon his tongue:
'No Earthly Parents I confess:
'I am doing my Father's business.'
When the rich learned Pharisee
Came to consult him secretly,
Upon his heart with Iron pen
He wrote, 'Ye must be born again.'
He was too proud to take a bribe;
He spoke with authority, not like a Scribe.
He says with most consummate Art,
'Follow me, I am meek & lowly of heart,'
As that is the only way to escape
The Miser's net & the Glutton's trap.
What can be done with such desperate Fools
Who follow after the Heathen Schools?
I was standing by when Jesus died;
What I call'd Humility, they call'd Pride.
He who loves his Enemies betrays his Friends;
This surely is not what Jesus intends,
But the sneaking Pride of Heroic Schools,
And the Scribes' & Pharisees' Virtuous Rules;
For he acts with honest, triumphant Pride,
And this is the cause that Jesus died.
He did not die with Christian Ease,
Asking pardon of his Enemies:
If he had, Cai(a)phas would forgive;
Sneaking submission can always live.
He had only to say that God was the devil,
And the devil was God, like a Christian Civil:
Mild Christian regrets to the devil confess

For affronting him thrice in the Wilderness;
He had soon been bloody Caesar's Elf,
And at last he would have been Caesar himself.
Like dr. Priestly & Bacon & Newton –
Poor Spiritual Knowledge is not worth a button!
For thus the Gospel Sir Isaac confutes:
'God can only be known by his Attributes;
'And as for the Indwelling of the Holy Ghost
'Or of Christ & his Father, it's all a boast
'And Pride & Vanity of the imagination,
'That disdains to follow this World's Fashion.'
To teach doubt & Experiment
Certainly was not what Christ meant.
What was he doing all that time,
From twelve years old to manly prime?
Was he then Idle, or the Less
About his Father's business?
Or was his wisdom held in scorn
Before his wrath began to burn
In Miracles throughout the Land,
That quite unnerv'd Caiaphas' hand?
If he had been Antichrist, Creeping Jesus,
He'd have done any thing to please us –
Gone sneaking into Synagogues
And not us'd the Elders & Priests like dogs,
But Humble as a Lamb or Ass
Obey'd himself to Caiaphas.
God wants not Man to Humble himself:
This is the trick of the ancient Elf.
This is the Race that Jesus ran:
Humble to God, Haughty to Man,
Cursing the Rulers before the People
Even to the temple's highest Steeple;
And when he Humbled himself to God,
Then descended the Cruel Rod.

'If thou humblest thyself, thou humblest me;
'Thou also dwell'st in Eternity.
'Thou art a Man, God is no more,
'Thy own humanity learn to adore,
'For that is my Spirit of Life.
'Awake, arise to Spiritual Strife
'And thy Revenge abroad display
'In terrors at the Last Judgment day.
'God's Mercy & Long Suffering
'Is but the Sinner to Judgment to bring.
'Thou on the Cross for them shalt pray
'And take Revenge at the Last Day.
'This Corporeal life's a fiction
'And is made up of Contradiction.'
Jesus replied & thunders hurl'd:
'I never will Pray for the World.
'Once I did so when I pray'd in the Garden;
'I wish'd to take with me a Bodily Pardon.'
Can that which was of woman born
In the absence of the Morn,
When the Soul fell into Sleep
And Archangels round it weep,
Shooting out against the Light
Fibres of a deadly night,
Reasoning upon its own dark Fiction,
In doubt which is Self Contradiction?
Humility is only doubt,
And does the Sun & Moon blot out,
Rooting over with thorns & stems
The buried Soul & all its Gems.
This Life's dim Windows of the Soul
Distorts the Heavens from Pole to Pole
And leads you to Believe a Lie
When you see with, not thro', the Eye
That was born in a night to perish in a night,

When the Soul slept in the beams of Light
Was Jesus Chaste? or did he, &c.

*

Was Jesus Chaste? or did he
Give any Lessons of Chastity?
The morning blush'd fiery red:
Mary was found in Adulterous bed;
Earth groan'd beneath, & Heaven above
Trembled at discovery of Love.
Jesus was sitting in Moses' Chair,
They brought the trembling Woman There.
Moses commands she be stoned to death,
What was the sound of Jesus' breath?
He laid His hand on Moses' Law:
The Ancient Heavens, in Silent Awe
Writ with Curses from Pole to Pole,
All away began to roll:
The Earth trembling & Naked lay
In secret bed of Mortal Clay,
On Sinai felt the hand divine
Putting back the bloody shrine,
And she heard the breath of God
As she heard by Eden's flood:
'Good & Evil are no more!
'Sinai's trumpets, cease to roar!
'Cease, finger of God, to write!
'The Heavens are not clean in thy Sight.
'Thou art Good, & Thou Alone;
'Nor may the sinner cast one stone.
'To be Good only, is to be
'A God or else a Pharisee.
'Thou Angel of the Presence Divine
'That didst create this Body of Mine,

'Wherefore hast thou writ these Laws
'And Created Hell's dark jaws?
'My presence I will take from thee:
'A Cold Leper thou shalt be.
'Tho' thou wast so pure & bright
'That Heaven was Impure in thy Sight,
'Tho' thy Oath turn'd Heaven Pale,
'Tho' thy Covenant built Hell's Jail,
'Tho' thou didst all to Chaos roll
'With the Serpent for its soul,
'Still the breath Divine does move
'And the breath Divine is Love.
'Mary, Fear Not! Let me see
'The Seven Devils that torment thee:
'Hide not from my Sight thy Sin,
'That forgiveness thou maist win.
'Has no Man Condemned thee?'
'No Man, Lord:' 'then what is he
'Who shall Accuse thee? Come Ye forth,
'Fallen fiends of Heav'nly birth
'That have forgot your Ancient love
'And driven away my trembling Dove
'You shall bow before her feet;
'You shall lick the dust for Meat;
'And tho' you cannot Love, but Hate,
'Shall be beggars at Love's Gate.
'What was thy love? Let me see it;
'Was it love or dark deceit?'
'Love too long from Me has fled;
''Twas dark deceit, to Earn my bread;
''Twas Covet, or 'twas Custom, or
'Some trifle not worth caring for;
'That they may call a shame & Sin
'Love's temple that God dwelleth in,
'And hide in secret hidden Shrine

'The Naked Human form divine,
'And render that a Lawless thing
'On which the Soul Expands its wing.
'But this, O Lord, this was my Sin
'When first I let these Devils in
'In dark pretence to Chastity:
'Blaspheming Love, blaspheming thee.
'Thence Rose Secret Adulteries,
'And thence did Covet also rise.
'My sin thou hast forgiven me,
'Canst thou forgive my Blasphemy?
'Canst thou return to this dark Hell,
'And in my burning bosom dwell?
'And canst thou die that I may live?
'And canst thou Pity & forgive?'
Then Roll'd the shadowy Man away
From the Limbs of Jesus, to make them his prey,
An Ever devouring appetite
Glittering with festering Venoms bright,
Crying, 'Crucify this cause of distress,
'Who don't keep the secrets of Holiness!
'All Mental Powers by Diseases we bind,
'But he heals the deaf & the Dumb & the Blind.
'Whom God has afflicted for Secret Ends,
'He Comforts & Heals & calls them Friends.'
But, when Jesus was Crucified,
Then was perfected his glitt'ring pride:
In three Nights he devour'd his prey,
And still he devours the Body of Clay;
For dust & Clay is the Serpent's meat,
Which never was made for Man to Eat.

*

I am sure This Jesus will not do
Either for Englishman or Jew.

*

Seeing this False Christ, In fury & Passion
I made my Voice heard all over the Nation.
What are those, &c.

   The rest of this passage is lost.

      *

This was spoke by My Spectre to Voltaire, Bacon, &c

Did Jesus teach doubt? or did he
Give any lessons of Philosophy,
Charge Visionaries with deceiving,
Or call Men wise for not Believing?

      *

Was Jesus Born of a Virgin Pure
With narrow Soul & looks demure?
If he intended to take on Sin
The Mother should an Harlot been,
Just such a one as Magdalen
With seven devils in her Pen;
Or were Jew Virgins still more Curst,
And more sucking devils nurst?
Or what was it which he took on
That he might bring Salvation?
A Body subject to be Tempted,
From neither pain nor grief Exempted?
Or such a body as might not feel
The passions that with Sinners deal?
Yes, but they say he never fell.
Ask Caiaphas; for he can tell.
'He mock'd the Sabbath, & he mock'd
'The Sabbath's God, & he unlock'd
'The Evil spirits from their Shrines,
'And turn'd Fishermen to Divines;
'O'erturn'd the Tent of Secret Sins,
'& its Golden cords & Pins –

''Tis the Bloody Shrine of War
'Pinn'd around from Star to Star,
'Halls of justice, hating Vice,
'Where the devil Combs his lice.
'He turn'd the devils into Swine
'That he might tempt the Jews to dine;
'Since which, a Pig has got a look
'That for a Jew may be mistook.
'"Obey your parents." – What says he?
'"Woman, what have I to do with thee?
'"No Earthly Parents I confess:
'"I am doing my Father's Business."
'He scorn'd Earth's Parents, scorn'd Earth's God,
'And mock'd the one & the other's Rod;
'His Seventy Disciples sent
'Against Religion & Government:
'They by the Sword of Justice fell
'And him their Cruel Murderer tell.
'He left his Father's trade to roam
'A wand'ring Vagrant without Home;
'And thus he others' labour stole
'That he might live above Controll.
'The Publicans & Harlots he
'Selected for his Company,
'And from the Adulteress turn'd away
'God's righteous Law, that lost its Prey.'

THE BOOK OF THEL

Etched 1789

Thel's Motto

Does the Eagle know what is in the pit?
Or wilt thou go ask the Mole?
Can Wisdom be put in a silver rod?
Or Love in a golden bowl?

I

The daughters of Mne Seraphim led round their sunny
    flocks,
All but the youngest; she in paleness sought the secret air,
To fade away like morning beauty from her mortal day:
Down by the river of Adona her soft voice is heard,
And thus her gentle lamentation falls like morning dew:

'O life of this our spring! why fades the lotus of the water,
'Why fade these children of the spring, born but to smile &
    fall?
'Ah! Thel is like a wat'ry bow, and like a parting cloud;
'Like a reflection in a glass, like shadows in the water,
'Like dreams of infants, like a smile upon an infant's face;
'Like the dove's voice; like transient day; like music in the
    air.
'Ah! gentle may I lay me down, and gentle rest my head,
'And gentle sleep the sleep of death, and gentle hear the
    voice
'Of him that walketh in the garden in the evening time.'

The Lilly of the valley, breathing in the humble grass,
Answer'd the lovely maid and said: 'I am a wat'ry weed,
'And I am very small and love to dwell in lowly vales;

THE BOOK OF THEL

'So weak, the gilded butterfly scarce perches on my head.
'Yet I am visited from heaven, and he that smiles on all
'Walks in the valley and each morn over me spreads his
      hand,
'Saying, "Rejoice, thou humble grass, thou new-born lilly
      flower,
'"Thou gentle maid of silent valleys and of modest brooks;
'"For thou shalt be clothed in light, and fed with morning
      manna,
'"Till summer's heat melts thee beside the fountains and
      the springs
'"To flourish in eternal vales." Then why should Thel com-
      plain?
'Why should the mistress of the vales of Har utter a sigh?'

She ceas'd & smil'd in tears, then sat down in her silver
      shrine.

Thel answer'd: 'O thou little virgin of the peaceful valley,
'Giving to those that cannot crave, the voiceless, the o'er-
      tired;
'Thy breath doth nourish the innocent lamb, he smells thy
      milky garments,
'He crops thy flowers while thou sittest smiling in his face,
'Wiping his mild and meekin' mouth from all contagious
      taints.
'Thy wine doth purify the golden honey; thy perfume,
'Which thou dost scatter on every little blade of grass that
      springs,
'Revives the milked cow, & tames the fire-breathing steed.
'But Thel is like a faint cloud kindled at the rising sun:
'I vanish from my pearly throne, and who shall find my
      place?'

'Queen of the vales,' the Lilly answer'd, 'ask the tender
      cloud,

'And it shall tell thee why it glitters in the morning sky,
'And why it scatters its bright beauty thro' the humid air.
'Descend, O little Cloud, & hover before the eyes of Thel.'

The Cloud descended, and the Lilly bow'd her modest head
And went to mind her numerous charge among the verdant
    grass.

II

'O little Cloud,' the virgin said, 'I charge thee tell to me
'Why thou complainest not when in one hour thou fade
    away:
'Then we shall seek thee, but not find. Ah! Thel is like to
    thee:
'I pass away: yet I complain, and no one hears my voice.'

The Cloud then shew'd his golden head & his bright form
    emerg'd,
Hovering and glittering on the air before the face of Thel.
'O virgin, know'st thou not our steeds drink of the golden
    springs
'Where Luvah doth renew his horses? Look'st thou on my
    youth,
'And fearest thou, because I vanish and am seen no more,
'Nothing remains? O maid, I tell thee, when I pass away
'It is to tenfold life, to love, to peace and rapture holy:
'Unseen descending, weigh my light wings upon balmy
    flowers,
'And court the fair-eyed dew to take me to her shining tent:
'The weeping virgin, trembling kneels before the risen sun,
'Till we arise link'd in a golden band and never part,
'But walk united, bearing food to all our tender flowers.'

'Dost thou, O little Cloud? I fear that I am not like thee,
'For I walk thro' the vales of Har, and smell the sweetest
    flowers,

'But I feed not the little flowers; I hear the warbling birds,
'But I feed not the warbling birds; they fly and seek their
    food:
'But Thel delights in these no more, because I fade away;
'And all shall say, "Without a use this shining woman liv'd,
'"Or did she only live to be at death the food of worms?"'

The Cloud reclin'd upon his airy throne and answer'd thus:

'Then if thou art the food of worms, O virgin of the skies,
'How great thy use, how great thy blessing! Every thing
    that lives
'Lives not alone nor for itself. Fear not, and I will call
'The weak worm from its lowly bed, and thou shalt hear its
    voice.
'Come forth, worm of the silent valley, to thy pensive
    queen.'

The helpless worm arose, and sat upon the Lilly's leaf,
And the bright Cloud sail'd on, to find his partner in the
    vale.

III

Then Thel astonish'd view'd the Worm upon its dewy bed.

'Art thou a Worm? Image of weakness, art thou but a
    Worm?
'I see thee like an infant wrapped in the Lilly's leaf.
'Ah! weep not, little voice, thou canst not speak, but thou
    canst weep.
'Is this a Worm? I see thee lay helpless & naked, weeping,
'And none to answer, none to cherish thee with mother's
    smiles.'

The Clod of Clay heard the Worm's voice & rais'd her pity-
    ing head:
She bow'd over the weeping infant, and her life exhal'd
In milky fondness: then on Thel she fix'd her humble eyes.

'O beauty of the vales of Har! we live not for ourselves.

'Thou seest me the meanest thing, and so I am indeed.

'My bosom of itself is cold, and of itself is dark;

'But he, that loves the lowly, pours his oil upon my head,

'And kisses me, and binds his nuptial bands around my breast,

'And says: "Thou mother of my children, I have loved thee

'"And I have given thee a crown that none can take away."

'But how this is, sweet maid, I know not, and I cannot know;

'I ponder, and I cannot ponder; yet I live and love.'

The daughter of beauty wip'd her pitying tears with her white veil,

And said: 'Alas! I knew not this, and therefore did I weep.

'That God would love a Worm I knew, and punish the evil foot

'That wilful bruis'd its helpless form; but that he cherish'd it

'With milk and oil I never knew, and therefore did I weep;

'And I complain'd in the mild air, because I fade away,

'And lay me down in thy cold bed, and leave my shining lot.'

'Queen of the vales,' the matron Clay answer'd, 'I heard thy sighs,

'And all thy moans flew o'er my roof, but I have call'd them down.

'Wilt thou, O Queen, enter my house? 'Tis given thee to enter

And to return: fear nothing, enter with thy virgin feet.'

IV

The eternal gates' terrific porter lifted the northern bar:

Thel enter'd in & saw the secrets of the land unknown.

She saw the couches of the dead, & where the fibrous roots
Of every heart on earth infixes deep its restless twists:
A land of sorrows & of tears where never smile was seen.

She wander'd in the land of clouds thro' valleys dark, list'n-
    ing
Dolours & lamentations; waiting oft beside a dewy grave
She stood in silence, list'ning to the voices of the ground,
Till to her own grave plot she came, & there she sat down,
And heard this voice of sorrow breathed from the hollow
    pit.

'Why cannot the Ear be closed to its own destruction?
'Or the glist'ning Eye to the poison of a smile?
'Why are Eyelids stor'd with arrows ready drawn,
'Where a thousand fighting men in ambush lie?
'Or an Eye of gifts & graces show'ring fruits & coined gold?
'Why a Tongue impress'd with honey from every wind?
'Why an Ear, a whirlpool fierce to draw creations in?
'Why a Nostril wide inhaling terror, trembling, & affright?
'Why a tender curb upon the youthful burning boy?
'Why a little curtain of flesh on the bed of our desire?'

The Virgin started from her seat, & with a shriek
Fled back unhinder'd till she came into the vales of Har.

THE END

THE MARRIAGE OF HEAVEN
AND HELL

Etched about 1793

The Argument

Rintrah roars & shakes his fires in the burden'd air;
Hungry clouds swag on the deep.

Once meek, and in a perilous path,
The just man kept his course along
The vale of death.
Roses are planted where thorns grow,
And on the barren heath
Sing the honey bees.

Then the perilous path was planted,
And a river and a spring
On every cliff and tomb,
And on the bleached bones
Red clay brought forth;

Till the villain left the paths of ease,
To walk in perilous paths, and drive
The just man into barren climes.

Now the sneaking serpent walks
In mild humility,
And the just man rages in the wilds
Where lions roam.

Rintrah roars & shakes his fires in the burden'd air;
Hungry clouds swag on the deep.

*

As a new heaven is begun, and it is now thirty-three years since its advent, the Eternal Hell revives. And lo! Swedenborg is the Angel sitting at the tomb: his writings are the linen clothes folded up. Now is the dominion of Edom, & the return of Adam into Paradise. See Isaiah xxxiv & xxxv Chap.

Without Contraries is no progression. Attraction and Repulsion, Reason and Energy, Love and Hate, are necessary to Human existence.

From these contraries spring what the religious call Good & Evil. Good is the passive that obeys Reason. Evil is the active springing from Energy.

Good is Heaven. Evil is Hell.

The Voice of the Devil

All Bibles or sacred codes have been the causes of the following Errors:

1. That Man has two real existing principles: Viz: a Body & a Soul.

2. That Energy, call'd Evil, is alone from the Body; & that Reason, call'd Good, is alone from the Soul.

3. That God will torment Man in Eternity for following his Energies.

But the following Contraries to these are True:

1. Man has no Body distinct from his Soul; for that call'd Body is a portion of Soul discern'd by the five Senses, the chief inlets of Soul in this age.

2. Energy is the only life, and is from the Body; and Reason is the bound or outward circumference of Energy.

3. Energy is Eternal Delight.

*

Those who restrain desire, do so because theirs is weak enough to be restrained; and the restrainer or reason usurps its place & governs the unwilling.

And being restrain'd, it by degrees becomes passive, till it is only the shadow of desire.

The history of this is written in Paradise Lost, & the Governor or Reason is call'd Messiah.

And the original Archangel, or possessor of the command of the heavenly host, is call'd the Devil or Satan, and his children are call'd Sin & Death.

But in the Book of Job, Milton's Messiah is call'd Satan.

For this history has been adopted by both parties.

It indeed appear'd to Reason as if Desire was cast out; but the Devil's account is, that the Messiah fell, & formed a heaven of what he stole from the Abyss.

This is shewn in the Gospel, where he prays to the Father to send the comforter, or Desire, that Reason may have Ideas to build on; the Jehovah of the Bible being no other than he who dwells in flaming fire.

Know that after Christ's death, he became Jehovah.

But in Milton, the Father is Destiny, the Son a Ratio of the five senses, & the Holy-ghost Vacuum!

Note: The reason Milton wrote in fetters when he wrote of Angels & God, and at liberty when of Devils & Hell, is because he was a true Poet and of the Devil's party without knowing it.

A Memorable Fancy

As I was walking among the fires of hell, delighted with the enjoyments of Genius, which to Angels look like torment and insanity, I collected some of their Proverbs; thinking that as the sayings used in a nation mark its character, so the Proverbs of Hell show the nature of Infernal wisdom better than any description of buildings or garments.

When I came home: on the abyss of the five senses, where a flat sided steep frowns over the present world, I saw a mighty Devil folded in black clouds, hovering on the sides of the rock: with corroding fires he wrote the following sentence now perceived by the minds of men, & read by them on earth:

How do you know but ev'ry Bird that cuts the airy way,
Is an immense world of delight, clos'd by your senses five?

Proverbs of Hell

In seed time learn, in harvest teach, in winter enjoy.
Drive your cart and your plow over the bones of the dead.
The road of excess leads to the palace of wisdom.
Prudence is a rich, ugly old maid courted by Incapacity.
He who desires but acts not, breeds pestilence.
The cut worm forgives the plow.
Dip him in the river who loves water.
A fool sees not the same tree that a wise man sees.
He whose face gives no light, shall never become a star.
Eternity is in love with the productions of time.
The busy bee has no time for sorrow.
The hours of folly are measur'd by the clock; but of wisdom, no clock can measure.
All wholesome food is caught without a net or a trap.
Bring out number, weight & measure in a year of dearth.
No bird soars too high, if he soars with his own wings.
A dead body revenges not injuries.
The most sublime act is to set another before you.
If the fool would persist in his folly he would become wise.
Folly is the cloke of knavery.
Shame is Pride's cloke.
Prisons are built with stones of Law, Brothels with bricks of Religion.

The pride of the peacock is the glory of God.

The lust of the goat is the bounty of God.

The wrath of the lion is the wisdom of God.

The nakedness of woman is the work of God.

Excess of sorrow laughs. Excess of joy weeps.

The roaring of lions, the howling of wolves, the raging of the stormy sea, and the destructive sword, are portions of eternity, too great for the eye of man.

The fox condemns the trap, not himself.

Joys impregnate. Sorrows bring forth.

Let man wear the fell of the lion, woman the fleece of the sheep.

The bird a nest, the spider a web, man friendship.

The selfish, smiling fool, & the sullen, frowning fool shall be both thought wise, that they may be a rod.

What is now proved was once only imagin'd.

The rat, the mouse, the fox, the rabbet watch the roots; the lion, the tyger, the horse, the elephant watch the fruits.

The cistern contains; the fountain overflows.

One thought fills immensity.

Always be ready to speak your mind, and a base man will avoid you.

Every thing possible to be believed is an image of truth.

The eagle never lost so much time as when he submitted to learn of the crow.

The fox provides for himself, but God provides for the lion.

Think in the morning. Act in the noon. Eat in the evening. Sleep in the night.

He who has suffer'd you to impose on him, knows you.

As the plow follows words, so God rewards prayers.

The tygers of wrath are wiser than the horses of instruction.

Expect poison from the standing water.

You never know what is enough unless you know what is more than enough.

Listen to the fool's reproach! it is a kingly title!

The eyes of fire, the nostrils of air, the mouth of water, the beard of earth.

The weak in courage is strong in cunning.

The apple tree never asks the beech how he shall grow; nor the lion, the horse, how he shall take his prey.

The thankful reciever bears a plentiful harvest.

If others had not been foolish, we should be so.

The soul of sweet delight can never be defil'd.

When thou seest an Eagle, thou seest a portion of Genius; lift up thy head!

As the catterpiller chooses the fairest leaves to lay her eggs on, so the priest lays his curse on the fairest joys.

To create a little flower is the labour of ages.

Damn braces: Bless relaxes.

The best wine is the oldest, the best water the newest.

Prayers plow not! Praises reap not!

Joys laugh not! Sorrows weep not!

The head Sublime, the heart Pathos, the genitals Beauty, the hands & feet Proportion.

As the air to a bird or the sea to a fish, so is contempt to the contemptible.

The crow wish'd every thing was black, the owl that every thing was white.

Exuberance is Beauty.

If the lion was advised by the fox, he would be cunning.

Improvement makes strait roads; but the crooked roads without Improvement are roads of Genius.

Sooner murder an infant in its cradle than nurse unacted desires.

Where man is not, nature is barren.

Truth can never be told so as to be understood, and not be believ'd.

Enough! or Too much.

*

The ancient Poets animated all sensible objects with Gods or Geniuses, calling them by the names and adorning them with the properties of woods, rivers, mountains, lakes, cities, nations, and whatever their enlarged & numerous senses could percieve.

And particularly they studied the genius of each city & country, placing it under its mental deity;

Till a system was formed, which some took advantage of, & enslav'd the vulgar by attempting to realize or abstract the mental deities from their objects: thus began Priesthood;

Choosing forms of worship from poetic tales.

And at length they pronounc'd that the Gods had order'd such things.

Thus men forgot that All deities reside in the human breast.

A Memorable Fancy

The Prophets Isaiah and Ezekiel dined with me, and I asked them how they dared so roundly to assert that God spoke to them; and whether they did not think at the time that they would be misunderstood, & so be the cause of imposition.

Isaiah answer'd: 'I saw no God, nor heard any, in a 'finite organical perception; but my senses discover'd the 'infinite in everything, and as I was then perswaded, & 'remain confirm'd, that the voice of honest indignation is 'the voice of God, I cared not for consequences, but wrote.'

Then I asked: 'does a firm perswasion that a thing is so, 'make it so?'

He replied: 'All poets believe that it does, & in ages of 'imagination this firm perswasion removed mountains; but 'many are not capable of a firm perswasion of any thing.'

Then Ezekiel said: 'The philosophy of the east taught the 'first principles of human perception: some nations held one

'principle for the origin, and some another: we of Israel
'taught that the Poetic Genius (as you now call it) was the
'first principle and all the others merely derivative, which
'was the cause of our despising the Priests & Philosophers of
'other countries, and prophecying that all Gods would at
'last be proved to originate in ours & to be the tributaries of
'the Poetic Genius; it was this that our great poet, King
'David, desired so fervently & invokes so pathetic'ly, saying
'by this he conquers enemies & governs kingdoms; and we
'so loved our God, that we cursed in his name all the deities
'of surrounding nations, and asserted that they had rebelled:
'from these opinions the vulgar came to think that all
'nations would at last be subject to the jews.

'This,' said he, 'like all firm perswasions, is come to pass;
'for all nations believe the jews' code and worship the jews'
'god, and what greater subjection can be?'

I heard this with some wonder, & must confess my own
conviction. After dinner I ask'd Isaiah to favour the world
with his lost works; he said none of equal value was lost.
Ezekiel said the same of his.

I also asked Isaiah what made him go naked and bare-
foot three years? he answer'd: 'the same that made our
'friend Diogenes, the Grecian.'

I then asked Ezekiel why he eat dung, & lay so long on
his right & left side? he answer'd, 'the desire of raising
'other men into a perception of the infinite: this the North
'American tribes practise, & is he honest who resists his
'genius or conscience only for the sake of present ease or
'gratification?'

*

The ancient tradition that the world will be consumed in
fire at the end of six thousand years is true, as I have heard
from Hell.

For the cherub with his flaming sword is hereby commanded to leave his guard at tree of life; and when he does, the whole creation will be consumed and appear infinite and holy, whereas it now appears finite & corrupt.

This will come to pass by an improvement of sensual enjoyment.

But first the notion that man has a body distinct from his soul is to be expunged; this I shall do by printing in the infernal method, by corrosives, which in Hell are salutary and medicinal, melting apparent surfaces away, and displaying the infinite which was hid.

If the doors of perception were cleansed every thing would appear to man as it is, infinite.

For man has closed himself up, till he sees all things thro' narrow chinks of his cavern.

A Memorable Fancy

I was in a Printing house in Hell, & saw the method in which knowledge is transmitted from generation to generation.

In the first chamber was a Dragon-Man, clearing away the rubbish from a cave's mouth; within, a number of Dragons were hollowing the cave.

In the second chamber was a Viper folding round the rock & the cave, and others adorning it with gold, silver and precious stones.

In the third chamber was an Eagle with wings and feathers of air: he caused the inside of the cave to be infinite; around were numbers of Eagle-like men who built palaces in the immense cliffs.

In the fourth chamber were Lions of flaming fire, raging around & melting the metals into living fluids.

In the fifth chamber were Unnam'd forms, which cast the metals into the expanse.

There they were reciev'd by Men who occupied the sixth chamber, and took the forms of books & were arranged in libraries.

*

The Giants who formed this world into its sensual existence, and now seem to live in it in chains, are in truth the causes of its life & the sources of all activity; but the chains are the cunning of weak and tame minds which have power to resist energy; according to the proverb, the weak in courage is strong in cunning.

Thus one portion of being is the Prolific, the other the Devouring; to the Devourer it seems as if the producer was in his chains; but it is not so, he only takes portions of existence and fancies that the whole.

But the Prolific would cease to be Prolific unless the Devourer, as a sea, reciev'd the excess of his delights.

Some will say: 'Is not God alone the Prolific?' I answer: 'God only Acts & Is, in existing beings or Men.'

These two classes of men are always upon earth, & they should be enemies: whoever tries to reconcile them seeks to destroy existence.

Religion is an endeavour to reconcile the two.

Note: Jesus Christ did not wish to unite, but to separate them, as in the Parable of sheep and goats! & he says: 'I came not to send Peace, but a Sword.'

Messiah or Satan or Tempter was formerly thought to be one of the Antediluvians who are our Energies.

A Memorable Fancy

An Angel came to me and said: 'O pitiable foolish young 'man! O horrible! O dreadful state! consider the hot 'burning dungeon thou art preparing for thyself to all 'eternity, to which thou art going in such career.'

I said: 'Perhaps you will be willing to shew me my 'eternal lot, & we will contemplate together upon it, and 'see whether your lot or mine is most desirable.'

So he took me thro' a stable & thro' a church & down into the church vault, at the end of which was a mill: thro' the mill we went, and came to a cave: down the winding cavern we groped our tedious way, till a void boundless as a nether sky appear'd beneath us, & we held by the roots of trees and hung over this immensity; but I said: 'if you 'please, we will commit ourselves to this void, and see 'whether providence is here also: if you will not, I will:' but he answer'd: 'do not presume, O young man, but as 'we here remain, behold thy lot which will soon appear 'when the darkness passes away.'

So I remain'd with him, sitting in the twisted root of an oak; he was suspended in a fungus, which hung with the head downward into the deep.

By degrees we beheld the infinite Abyss, fiery as the smoke of a burning city; beneath us, at an immense distance, was the sun, black but shining; round it were fiery tracks on which revolv'd vast spiders, crawling after their prey, which flew, or rather swum, in the infinite deep, in the most terrific shapes of animals sprung from corruption; & the air was full of them, & seem'd composed of them: these are Devils, and are called Powers of the air. I now asked my companion which was my eternal lot? he said: 'between 'the black & white spiders.'

But now, from between the black & white spiders, a cloud and fire burst and rolled thro' the deep, black'ning all beneath, so that the nether deep grew black as a sea, & rolled with a terrible noise; beneath us was nothing now to be seen but a black tempest, till looking east between the clouds & the waves, we saw a cataract of blood mixed with fire, and not many stones' throw from us appear'd and sunk again the scaly fold of a monstrous serpent; at last, to the east, distant about three degrees, appear'd a fiery crest above the waves: slowly it reared like a ridge of golden rocks, till we discover'd two globes of crimson fire, from which the sea fled away in clouds of smoke; and now we saw it was the head of Leviathan; his forehead was divided into streaks of green & purple like those on a tyger's forehead: soon we saw his mouth & red gills hang just above the raging foam, tinging the black deep with beams of blood, advancing toward us with all the fury of a spiritual existence.

My friend the Angel climb'd up from his station into the mill: I remain'd alone; & then this appearance was no more, but I found myself sitting on a pleasant bank beside a river by moonlight, hearing a harper, who sung to the harp; & his theme was: 'The man who never alters his 'opinion is like standing water, & breeds reptiles of the 'mind.'

But I arose and sought for the mill, & there I found my Angel, who, surprised, asked me how I escaped?

I answer'd: 'All that we saw was owing to your meta-'physics; for when you ran away, I found myself on a bank 'by moonlight hearing a harper. But now we have seen my 'eternal lot, shall I shew you yours?' he laugh'd at my proposal; but I by force suddenly caught him in my arms, & flew westerly thro' the night, till we were elevated above the earth's shadow; then I flung myself with him directly into the body of the sun; here I clothed myself in white, & taking in my hand Swedenborg's volumes, sunk from the glorious clime, and passed all the planets till we came to saturn: here I stay'd to rest, & then leap'd into the void between saturn & the fixed stars.

'Here,' said I, 'is your lot, in this space – if space it may 'be call'd.' Soon we saw the stable and the church, & I took him to the altar and open'd the Bible, and lo! it was a deep pit, into which I descended, driving the Angel before me; soon we saw seven houses of brick; one we enter'd; in it were a number of monkeys, baboons, & all of that species, chain'd by the middle, grinning and snatching at one another, but withheld by the shortness of their chains: however, I saw that they sometimes grew numerous, and then the weak were caught by the strong, and with a grinning aspect, first coupled with, & then devour'd, by plucking off first one limb and then another, till the body was left a helpless trunk; this, after grinning & kissing it with seeming fondness, they devour'd too; and here & there I saw one savourily picking the flesh off his own tail; as the stench terribly annoy'd us both, we went into the mill, & I in my hand brought the skeleton of a body, which in the mill was Aristotle's Analytics.

So the Angel said: 'thy phantasy has imposed upon me, '& thou oughtest to be ashamed.'

I answer'd: 'we impose on one another, & it is but lost 'time to converse with you whose works are only Analytics.'

*

Opposition is true Friendship.

*

I have always found that Angels have the vanity to speak of themselves as the only wise; this they do with a confident insolence sprouting from systematic reasoning.

Thus Swedenborg boasts that what he writes is new: tho' it is only the Contents or Index of already publish'd books.

A man carried a monkey about for a shew, & because he was a little wiser than the monkey, grew vain, and conciev'd himself as much wiser than seven men. It is so with Swedenborg: he shews the folly of churches, & exposes hypocrites, till he imagines that all are religious, & himself the single one on earth that ever broke a net.

Now hear a plain fact: Swedenborg has not written one new truth. Now hear another: he has written all the old falsehoods.

And now hear the reason. He conversed with Angels who are all religious, & conversed not with Devils who all hate religion, for he was incapable thro' his conceited notions.

Thus Swedenborg's writings are a recapitulation of all superficial opinions, and an analysis of the more sublime – but no further.

Have now another plain fact. Any man of mechanical talents may, from the writings of Paracelsus or Jacob Behmen, produce ten thousand volumes of equal value with Swedenborg's, and from those of Dante or Shakespear an infinite number.

But when he has done this, let him not say that he knows better than his master, for he only holds a candle in sunshine.

A Memorable Fancy

Once I saw a Devil in a flame of fire, who arose before an Angel that sat on a cloud, and the Devil utter'd these words: 'The worship of God is: Honouring his gifts in other men, 'each according to his genius, and loving the greatest men 'best: those who envy or calumniate great men hate God: 'for there is no other God.'

The Angel hearing this became almost blue; but mastering himself he grew yellow, & at last white, pink, & smiling, and then replied:

'Thou Idolater! is not God One? & is not he visible in 'Jesus Christ? and has not Jesus Christ given his sanction to 'the law of ten commandments? and are not all other men 'fools, sinners, & nothings?'

The Devil answer'd: 'bray a fool in a morter with wheat, 'yet shall not his folly be beaten out of him; if Jesus Christ

'is the greatest man, you ought to love him in the greatest
'degree; now hear how he has given his sanction to the law
'of ten commandments: did he not mock at the sabbath,
'and so mock the sabbath's God? murder those who were
'murder'd because of him? turn away the law from the
'woman taken in adultery? steal the labour of others to sup-
'port him? bear false witness when he omitted making a
'defence before Pilate? covet when he pray'd for his dis-
'ciples, and when he bid them shake off the dust of their feet
'against such as refused to lodge them? I tell you, no virtue
'can exist without breaking these ten commandments. Jesus
'was all virtue, and acted from impulse, not from rules.'

When he had so spoken, I beheld the Angel, who stretched
out his arms, embracing the flame of fire, & he was con-
sumed and arose as Elijah.

Note: This Angel, who is now become a Devil, is my
particular friend; we often read the Bible together in its
infernal or diabolical sense, which the world shall have if
they behave well.

I have also The Bible of Hell, which the world shall have
whether they will or no.

*

One Law for the Lion & Ox is Oppression.

A Song of Liberty

1. The Eternal Female groan'd! it was heard over all the
Earth.
2. Albion's coast is sick, silent; the American meadows
faint!
3. Shadows of Prophecy shiver along by the lakes and the
rivers, and mutter across the ocean: France, rend down thy
dungeon!
4. Golden Spain, burst the barriers of old Rome!

5. Cast thy keys, O Rome, into the deep down falling, even to eternity down falling,

6. And weep.

7. In her trembling hands she took the new born terror, howling.

8. On those infinite mountains of light, now barr'd out by the atlantic sea, the new born fire stood before the starry king!

9. Flag'd with grey brow'd snows and thunderous visages, the jealous wings wav'd over the deep.

10. The speary hand burned aloft, unbuckled was the shield; forth went the hand of jealousy among the flaming hair, and hurl'd the new born wonder thro' the starry night.

11. The fire, the fire is falling!

12. Look up! look up! O citizen of London, enlarge thy countenance! O Jew, leave counting gold! return to thy oil and wine. O African! black African! (go, winged thought, widen his forehead.)

13. The fiery limbs, the flaming hair, shot like the sinking sun into the western sea.

14. Wak'd from his eternal sleep, the hoary element roaring fled away.

15. Down rush'd, beating his wings in vain, the jealous king; his grey brow'd councellors, thunderous warriors, curl'd veterans, among helms, and shields, and chariots, horses, elephants, banners, castles, slings, and rocks.

16. Falling, rushing, ruining! buried in the ruins, on Urthona's dens;

17. All night beneath the ruins; then, their sullen flames faded, emerge round the gloomy King.

18. With thunder and fire, leading his starry hosts thro' the waste wilderness, he promulgates his ten commands, glancing his beamy eyelids over the deep in dark dismay,

19. Where the son of fire in his eastern cloud, while the morning plumes her golden breast,

20. Spurning the clouds written with curses, stamps the stony law to dust, loosing the eternal horses from the dens of night, crying:

EMPIRE IS NO MORE! AND NOW THE LION &
WOLF SHALL CEASE.

CHORUS

Let the Priests of the Raven of dawn no longer, in deadly black, with hoarse note curse the sons of joy. Nor his accepted brethren – whom, tyrant, he calls free – lay the bound or build the roof. Nor pale religious letchery call that virginity that wishes but acts not!

For every thing that lives is Holy.

AMERICA

A PROPHECY

Etched 1793

Preludium

The shadowy Daughter of Urthona stood before red Orc,
When fourteen suns had faintly journey'd o'er his dark
    abode:
His food she brought in iron baskets, his drink in cups of
    iron:
Crown'd with a helmet & dark hair the nameless female
    stood;
A quiver with its burning stores, a bow like that of night,
When pestilence is shot from heaven: no other arms she
    need!
Invulnerable tho' naked, save where clouds roll round her
    loins
Their awful folds in the dark air: silent she stood as night;
For never from her iron tongue could voice or sound arise,
But dumb till that dread day when Orc assay'd his fierce
    embrace.

'Dark Virgin,' said the hairy youth, 'thy father stern, ab-
    horr'd,
'Rivets my tenfold chains while still on high my spirit soars;
'Sometimes an eagle screaming in the sky, sometimes a lion
'Stalking upon the mountains, & sometimes a whale, I lash
'The raging fathomless abyss; anon a serpent folding
'Around the pillars of Urthona, and round thy dark limbs
'On the Canadian wilds I fold; feeble my spirit folds,
'For chain'd beneath I rend these caverns: when thou
    bringest food.

'I howl my joy, and my red eyes seek to behold thy face –
'In vain! these clouds roll to & fro, & hide thee from my
sight.'

Silent as despairing love, and strong as jealousy,
The hairy shoulders rend the links; free are the wrists of fire;
Round the terrific loins he siez'd the panting, struggling
womb;
It joy'd: she put aside her clouds & smiled her first-born
smile,
As when a black cloud shews its lightnings to the silent deep.

Soon as she saw the terrible boy, then burst the virgin cry:

'I know thee, I have found thee, & I will not let thee go:
'Thou art the image of God who dwells in darkness of
Africa,
'And thou art fall'n to give me life in regions of dark death.
'On my American plains I feel the struggling afflictions
'Endur'd by roots that writhe their arms into the nether
deep.
'I see a Serpent in Canada who courts me to his love,
'In Mexico an Eagle, and a Lion in Peru;
'I see a Whale in the South-sea, drinking my soul away.
'O what limb rending pains I feel! thy fire & my frost
'Mingle in howling pains, in furrows by thy lightnings rent.
'This is eternal death, and this the torment long foretold.'

A Prophecy

The Guardian Prince of Albion burns in his nightly tent:
Sullen fires across the Atlantic glow to America's shore,
Piercing the souls of warlike men who rise in silent night.
Washington, Franklin, Paine & Warren, Gates, Hancock &
Green

Meet on the coast glowing with blood from Albion's fiery
    Prince.

Washington spoke: 'Friends of America! look over the
    Atlantic sea;
'A bended bow is lifted in heaven, & a heavy iron chain
'Descends, link by link, from Albion's cliffs across the sea, to
    bind
'Brothers & sons of America till our faces pale and yellow,
'Heads deprest, voices weak, eyes downcast, hands work-
    bruis'd,
'Feet bleeding on the sultry sands, and the furrows of the
    whip
'Descend to generations that in future times forget.'

The strong voice ceas'd, for a terrible blast swept over the
    heaving sea:
The eastern cloud rent: on his cliffs stood Albion's wrathful
    Prince,
A dragon form, clashing his scales: at midnight he arose,
And flam'd red meteors round the land of Albion beneath;
His voice, his locks, his awful shoulders, and his glowing
    eyes
Appear to the Americans upon the cloudy night.

Solemn heave the Atlantic waves between the gloomy
    nations,
Swelling, belching from its deeps red clouds & raging fires.
Albion is sick! America faints! enrag'd the Zenith grew.
As human blood shooting its veins all round the orbed
    heaven,
Red rose the clouds from the Atlantic in vast wheels of
    blood,
And in the red clouds rose a Wonder o'er the Atlantic sea,
Intense! naked! a Human fire, fierce glowing, as the wedge
Of iron heated in the furnace: his terrible limbs were fire

With myriads of cloudy terrors, banners dark & towers
Surrounded: heat but not light went thro' the murky atmo-
  sphere.

The King of England looking westward trembles at the
  vision.

Albion's Angel stood beside the Stone of night, and saw
The terror like a comet, or more like the planet red
That once enclos'd the terrible wandering comets in its
  sphere.
Then, Mars, thou wast our center, & the planets three flew
  round
Thy crimson disk: so e'er the Sun was rent from thy red
  sphere.
The Spectre glow'd his horrid length staining the temple
  long
With beams of blood; & thus a voice came forth, and shook
  the temple:

'The morning comes, the night decays, the watchmen leave
  their stations;
'The grave is burst, the spices shed, the linen wrapped up;
'The bones of death, the cov'ring clay, the sinews shrunk &
  dry'd
'Reviving shake, inspiring move, breathing, awakening,
'Spring like redeemed captives when their bonds & bars
  are burst.
'Let the slave grinding at the mill run out into the field,
'Let him look up into the heavens & laugh in the bright air;
'Let the inchained soul, shut up in darkness and in sighing,
'Whose face has never seen a smile in thirty weary years,
'Rise and look out; his chains are loose, his dungeon doors
  are open;
'And let his wife and children return from the oppressor's
  scourge.

'They look behind at every step & believe it is a dream,
'Singing: "The sun has left his blackness & has found a
      fresher morning,
'"And the fair Moon rejoices in the clear & cloudless night;
'"For Empire is no more, and now the Lion & Wolf shall
      cease."'

In thunders ends the voice. Then Albion's Angel wrathful
      burnt
Beside the Stone of Night, and like the Eternal Lion's howl
In famine & war, reply'd: 'Art thou not Orc, who serpent-
      form'd
'Stands at the gate of Enitharmon to devour her children?
'Blasphemous Demon, Antichrist, hater of Dignities,
'Lover of wild rebellion, and transgressor of God's Law,
'Why dost thou come to Angel's eyes in this terrific form?'

The Terror answer'd: 'I am Orc, wreath'd round the ac-
      cursed tree:
'The times are ended; shadows pass, the morning 'gins to
      break;
'The fiery joy, that Urizen perverted to ten commands,
'What night he led the starry hosts thro' the wide wilder-
      ness,
'That stony law I stamp to dust; and scatter religion abroad
'To the four winds as a torn book, & none shall gather the
      leaves;
'But they shall rot on desart sands, & consume in bottomless
      deeps,
'To make the desarts blossom, & the deeps shrink to their
      fountains,
'And to renew the fiery joy, and burst the stony roof;
'That pale religious letchery, seeking Virginity,
'May find it in a harlot, and in coarse-clad honesty
'The undefil'd, tho' ravish'd in her cradle night and morn;

'For everything that lives is holy, life delights in life;
'Because the soul of sweet delight can never be defil'd.
'Fires inwrap the earthly globe, yet man is not consum'd;
'Amidst the lustful fires he walks; his feet become like brass,
'His knees and thighs like silver, & his breast and head like
   gold.'

'Sound! sound! my loud war-trumpets, & alarm my Thir-
   teen Angels!
'Loud howls the eternal Wolf! the eternal Lion lashes his
   tail!
'America is darken'd; and my punishing Demons, terrified,
'Crouch howling before their caverns deep, like skins dry'd
   in the wind.
'They cannot smite the wheat, nor quench the fatness of the
   earth;
'They cannot smite with sorrows, nor subdue the plow and
   spade;
'They cannot wall the city, nor moat round the castle of
   princes;
'They cannot bring the stubbed oak to overgrow the hills;
'For terrible men stand on the shores, & in their robes I see
'Children take shelter from the lightnings: there stands
   Washington
'And Paine and Warren with their foreheads rear'd toward
   the east.
'But clouds obscure my aged sight. A vision from afar!
'Sound! sound! my loud war-trumpets, & alarm my thir-
   teen Angels!
'Ah vision from afar! Ah rebel form that rent the ancient
'Heavens! Eternal Viper, self-renew'd, rolling in clouds,
'I see thee in thick clouds and darkness on America's shore,
'Writhing in pangs of abhorred birth; red flames the crest
   rebellious
'And eyes of death; the harlot womb, oft opened in vain,

'Heaves in enormous circles: now the times are return'd
   upon thee,
'Devourer of thy parent, now thy unutterable torment re-
   news.
'Sound! sound! my loud war trumpets, & alarm my thir-
   teen Angels!
'Ah terrible birth! a young one bursting! where is the
   weeping mouth,
'And where the mother's milk? instead, those ever-hissing
   jaws
'And parched lips drop with fresh gore: now roll thou in the
   clouds;
'Thy mother lays her length outstretch'd upon the shore
   beneath.
'Sound! sound! my loud war-trumpets, & alarm my thir-
   teen Angels!
'Loud howls the eternal Wolf! the eternal Lion lashes his
   tail!'

Thus wept the Angel voice, & as he wept, the terrible blasts
Of trumpets blew a loud alarm across the Atlantic deep.
No trumpets answer; no reply of clarions or of fifes:
Silent the Colonies remain and refuse the loud alarm.

On those vast shady hills between America & Albion's shore,
Now barr'd out by the Atlantic sea, call'd Atlantean hills,
Because from their bright summits you may pass to the Gol-
   den world,
An ancient palace, archetype of mighty Emperies,
Rears its immortal pinnacles, built in the forest of God
By Ariston, the king of beauty, for his stolen bride.

Here on their magic seats the thirteen Angels sat perturb'd
For clouds from the Atlantic hover o'er the solemn roof.

Fiery the Angels rose, & as they rose deep thunder roll'd

Around their shores, indignant burning with the fires of Orc;
And Boston's Angel cried aloud as they flew thro' the dark
night.

He cried: 'Why trembles honesty, and like a murderer
'Why seeks he refuge from the frowns of his immortal sta-
tion?
'Must the generous tremble & leave his joy to the idle, to
the pestilence,
'That mock him? who commanded this? what God? what
Angel?
'To keep the gen'rous from experience till the ungenerous
'Are unrestrain'd performers of the energies of nature;
'Till pity is become a trade, and generosity a science
'That men get rich by; & the sandy desert is giv'n to the
strong?
'What God is he writes laws of peace & clothes him in a
tempest?
'What pitying Angel lusts for tears and fans himself with
sighs?
'What crawling villain preaches abstinence & wraps him-
self
'In fat of lambs? no more I follow, no more obedience pay!'

So cried he, rending off his robe & throwing down his scepter
In sight of Albion's Guardian; and all the thirteen Angels
Rent off their robes to the hungry wind, & threw their
golden scepters
Down on the land of America; indignant they descended
Headlong from out their heav'nly heights, descending swift
as fires
Over the land; naked & flaming are their lineaments seen
In the deep gloom; by Washington & Paine & Warren they
stood;
And the flame folded, roaring fierce within the pitchy night

Before the Demon red, who burnt towards America,

In black smoke, thunders, and loud winds, rejoicing in its
terror,

Breaking in smoky wreaths from the wild deep & gath'ring
thick

In flames as of a furnace on the land from North to South,

What time the thirteen Governors that England sent, con-
vene

In Bernard's house; the flames cover'd the land, they rouze,
they cry;

Shaking their mental chains, they rush in fury to the sea

To quench their anguish; at the feet of Washington down
fall'n

They grovel on the sand and writhing lie, while all

The British soldiers thro' the thirteen states sent up a howl

Of anguish, threw their swords & muskets to the earth, &
ran

From their encampments and dark castles, seeking where to
hide

From the grim flames, and from the visions of Orc, in sight

Of Albion's Angel; who, enrag'd, his secret clouds open'd

From north to south and burnt outstretch'd on wings of
wrath, covering

The eastern sky, spreading his awful wings across the
heavens.

Beneath him roll'd his num'rous hosts, all Albion's Angels
camp'd

Darken'd the Atlantic mountains; & their trumpets shook
the valleys,

Arm'd with diseases of the earth to cast upon the Abyss,

Their numbers forty millions, must'ring in the eastern sky.

In the flames stood & view'd the armies drawn out in the
sky,

Washington, Franklin, Paine, & Warren, Allen, Gates &
Lee,

And heard the voice of Albion's Angel give the thunderous
    command;
His plagues, obedient to his voice, flew forth out of their
    clouds,
Falling upon America, as a storm to cut them off,
As a blight cuts the tender corn when it begins to appear.
Dark is the heaven above, & cold & hard the earth beneath;
And as a plague wind fill'd with insects cuts off man &
    beast,
And as a sea o'erwhelms a land in the day of an earthquake,
Fury! rage! madness! in a wind swept through America;
And the red flames of Orc, that folded roaring, fierce,
    around
The angry shores; and the fierce rushing of th'inhabitants
    together!
The citizens of New York close their books & lock their
    chests;
The mariners of Boston drop their anchors and unlade;
The scribe of Pennsylvania casts his pen upon the earth;
The builder of Virginia throws his hammer down in fear.

Then had America been lost, o'erwhelmed by the Atlantic,
And Earth had lost another portion of the infinite,
But all rush together in the night in wrath and raging fire.
The red fires rag'd! the plagues recoil'd! then roll'd they
    back with fury
On Albion's Angels: then the Pestilence began in streaks of
    red
Across the limbs of Albion's Guardian; the spotted plague
    smote Bristol's
And the Leprosy London's Spirit, sickening all their bands:
The millions sent up a howl of anguish and threw off their
    hammer'd mail,
And cast their swords & spears to earth, & stood, a naked
    multitude:

Albion's Guardian writhed in torment on the eastern sky,

Pale, quiv'ring toward the brain his glimmering eyes, teeth
      chattering,

Howling & shuddering, his legs quivering, convuls'd each
      muscle & sinew;

Sick'ning lay London's Guardian, and the ancient miterd
      York,

Their heads on snowy hills, their ensigns sick'ning in the sky.

The plagues creep on the burning winds driven by flames of
      Orc,

And by the fierce Americans rushing together in the night,

Driven o'er the Guardians of Ireland, and Scotland and
      Wales.

They, spotted with plagues, forsook the frontiers; & their
      banners, sear'd

With fires of hell, deform their ancient heavens with shame
      & woe.

Hid in his caves the Bard of Albion felt the enormous
      plagues,

And a cowl of flesh grew o'er his head, & scales on his back
      & ribs;

And, rough with black scales, all his Angels fright their
      ancient heavens.

The doors of marriage are open, and the Priests in rustling
      scales

Rush into reptile coverts, hiding from the fires of Orc,

That play around the golden roofs in wreaths of fierce de-
      sire,

Leaving the females naked and glowing with the lusts of
      youth.

For the female spirits of the dead, pining in bonds of reli-
      gion,

Run from their fetters reddening, & in long drawn arches
      sitting,

They feel the nerves of youth renew, and desire of ancient
    times
Over their pale limbs, as a vine when the tender grape
    appears.

Over the hills, the vales, the cities, rage the red flames fierce;
The Heavens melted from north to south; and Urizen, who
    sat
Above all heavens, in thunders wrap'd, emerg'd his leprous
    head
From out his holy shrine, his tears in deluge piteous
Falling into the deep sublime; flag'd with grey-brow'd
    snows
And thunderous visages, his jealous wings wav'd over the
    deep;
Weeping in dismal howling woe, he dark descended, howl-
    ing
Around the smitten bands, clothed in tears & trembling,
    shudd'ring cold.
His stored snows he poured forth, and his icy magazines
He open'd on the deep, and on the Atlantic sea white
    shiv'ring
Leprous his limbs, all over white, and hoary was his visage,
Weeping in dismal howlings before the stern Americans,
Hiding the Demon red with clouds & cold mists from the
    earth;
Till Angels & weak men twelve years should govern o'er the
    strong;
And then their end should come, when France reciev'd the
    Demon's light.

Stiff shudderings shook the heav'nly thrones! France, Spain,
    & Italy
In terror view'd the bands of Albion, and the ancient
    Guardians,
Fainting upon the elements, smitten with their own plagues.

They slow advance to shut the five gates of their law-built
      heaven,
Filled with blasting fancies and with mildews of despair,
With fierce disease and lust, unable to stem the fires of Orc.
But the five gates were consum'd, & their bolts and hinges
      melted;
And the fierce flames burnt round the heavens, & round the
      abodes of men.

FINIS

AMERICA

Cancelled plates etched about 1793

A Prophecy

The Guardian Prince of Albion burns in his nightly tent:
Sullen fires across the Atlantic glow to America's shore,
Piercing the souls of warlike men who rise in silent night.
Washington, Hancock, Paine & Warren, Gates, Franklin &
    Green
Meet on the coast glowing with blood from Albion's fiery
    Prince.
Washington spoke: 'Friends of America! look over the
    Atlantic sea;
'A bended bow in heaven is lifted, & heavy iron chain
'Descends, link by link, from Albion's cliffs across the sea, to
    bind
'Brothers & sons of America till our faces pale and yellow,
'Heads deprest, voices weak, eyes downcast, hands work-
    bruised,
'Feet bleeding on the sultry sands, & the furrows of the whip
'Descend to generations that in future times forget.'

The strong voice ceas'd, for a terrible blast swept over the
    heaving sea:
The eastern cloud rent: on his cliffs stood Albions fiery
    Prince,
A dragon form, clashing his scales: at midnight he arose,
And flam'd fierce meteors round the band of Albion be-
    neath;
His voice, his locks, his awful shoulders, & his glowing eyes
Reveal the dragon thro' the human; coursing swift as fire
To the close hall of counsel, where his Angel form renews.
In a sweet vale shelter'd with cedars, that eternal stretch

Their unmov'd branches, stood the hall, built when the
    moon shot forth,
In that dread night when Urizen call'd the stars round his
    feet;
Then burst the center from its orb, and found a place be-
    neath;
And Earth conglob'd, in narrow room, roll'd round its sul-
    phur Sun.
To this deep valley situated by the flowing Thames,
Where George the third holds council & his Lords & Com-
    mons meet,
Shut out from mortal sight the Angel came; the vale was
    dark
With clouds of smoke from the Atlantic, that in volumes
    roll'd
Between the mountains; dismal visions mope around the
    house
On chairs of iron, canopied with mystic ornaments
Of life by magic power condens'd; infernal forms art-bound
The council sat; all rose before the aged apparition,
His snowy beard that streams like lambent flames down his
    wide breast
Wetting with tears, & his white garments cast a wintry
    light.
Then, as arm'd clouds arise terrific round the northern drum,
The world is silent at the flapping of the folding banners.
So still terrors rent the house, as when the solemn globe
Launch'd to the unknown shore, while Sotha held the
    northern helm,
Till to that void it came & fell; so the dark house was rent.
The valley mov'd beneath! its shining pillars split in twain,
And its roofs crack across down falling on th' Angelic seats.

Then Albion's Angel rose resolv'd to the cove of armoury;
His shield that bound twelve demons & their cities in its orb

He took down from its trembling pillar; from its cavern
    deep,

His helm was brought by London's Guardian, & his thirsty
    spear

By the wise spirit of London's river; silent stood the King
    breathing damp mists,

And on his aged limbs they clasp'd the armour of terrible
    gold.

Infinite London's awful spires cast a dreadful cold

Even on rational things beneath and from the palace walls

Around Saint James's, chill & heavy, even to the city gate.

On the vast stone whose name is Truth he stood, his cloudy
    shield

Smote with his scepter, the scale bound orb loud howl'd;
    the pillar

Trembling sunk, an earthquake roll'd along the mossy pile.

In glitt'ring armour, swift as winds, intelligent as clouds

Four winged heralds mount the furious blasts & blow their
    trumps;

Gold, silver, brass & iron clangors clamoring rend the
    shores.

Like white clouds rising from the deeps his fifty-two armies

From the four cliffs of Albion rise, mustering around their
    Prince;

Angels of cities and of parishes and villages and families,

In armour as the nerves of wisdom, each his station holds.

In opposition dire, a warlike cloud, the myriads stood

In the red air before the Demon seen by mortal men,

Who call it Fancy, or shut the gates of sense, or in their
    chambers

Sleep like the dead. But like a constellation ris'n and blazing

Over the rugged ocean, so the Angels of Albion hung

Over the frowning shadow like an aged King in arms of
    gold,

Who wept over a den, in which his only son outstretch'd

By rebels' hands was slain; his white beard wav'd in the
wild wind.

On mountains & cliffs of snow the awful apparition hover'd,
And like the voices of religious dead heard in the mountains
When holy zeal scents the sweet valleys of ripe virgin bliss,
Such was the hollow voice that o'er America lamented.

THE SONG OF LOS

Etched 1795

Africa

I will sing you a song of Los, the Eternal Prophet:
He sung it to four harps at the tables of Eternity.
In heart-formed Africa.
Urizen faded! Ariston shudder'd!
And thus the Song began:

Adam stood in the garden of Eden
And Noah on the mountains of Ararat;
They saw Urizen give his Laws to the Nations
By the hands of the children of Los.

Adam shudder'd! Noah faded! black grew the sunny Afri-
can
When Rintrah gave Abstract Philosophy to Brama in the
East.
(Night spoke to the Cloud:
'Lo these Human form'd spirits, in smiling hipocrisy, War
'Against one another; so let them War on, slaves to the
Eternal Elements.')
Noah shrunk beneath the waters;
Abram fled in fires from Chaldea;
Moses beheld upon Mount Sinai forms of dark delusion.

To Trismegistus, Palamabron gave an abstract Law:
To Pythagoras, Socrates & Plato.

Times rolled on o'er all the sons of Har: time after time
Orc on Mount Atlas howl'd, chain'd down with the Chain
of Jealousy;
Then Oothoon hover'd over Judah & Jerusalem,

And Jesus heard her voice (a man of sorrows) he reciev'd
A Gospel from wretched Theotormon.

The human race began to wither, for the healthy built
Secluded places, fearing the joys of Love,
And the diseased only propagated.
So Antamon call'd up Leutha from her valleys of delight
And to Mahomet a loose Bible gave.
But in the North, to Odin, Sotha gave a Code of War,
Because of Diralada, thinking to reclaim his joy.

These were the Churches, Hospitals, Castles, Palaces,
Like nets & gins & traps to catch the joys of Eternity,
        And all the rest a desart;
Till, like a dream, Eternity was obliterated & erased.

Since that dread day when Har and Heva fled
Because their brethren & sisters liv'd in War & Lust;
And as they fled they shrunk
Into two narrow doleful forms
Creeping in reptile flesh upon
The bosom of the ground;
And all the vast of Nature shrunk
Before their shrunken eyes.

Thus the terrible race of Los & Enitharmon gave
Laws & Religions to the sons of Har, binding them more
And more to Earth, closing and restraining,
Till a Philosophy of Five Senses was complete.
Urizen wept & gave it into the hands of Newton & Locke.

Clouds roll heavy upon the Alps round Rousseau & Vol-
        taire,
And on the mountains of Lebanon round the deceased Gods
Of Asia, & on the desarts of Africa round the Fallen Angels
The Guardian Prince of Albion burns in his nightly tent.

Asia

The Kings of Asia heard
The howl rise up from Europe,
And each ran out from his Web,
From his ancient woven Den;
For the darkness of Asia was startled
At the thick-flaming, thought-creating fires of Orc.

And the Kings of Asia stood
And cried in bitterness of soul:

'Shall not the King call for Famine from the heath,
'Nor the Priest for Pestilence from the fen,
'To restrain, to dismay, to thin
'The inhabitants of mountain and plain,
'In the day of full-feeding prosperity
'And the night of delicious songs?

'Shall not the Councellor throw his curb
'Of Poverty on the laborious,
'To fix the price of labour,
'To invent allegoric riches?

'And the privy admonishers of men
'Call for fires in the City,
'For heaps of smoking ruins
'In the night of prosperity & wantonness?

'To turn man from his path,
'To restrain the child from the womb,
'To cut off the bread from the city,
'That the remnant may learn to obey,

'That the pride of the heart may fail,
'That the lust of the eyes may be quench'd,
'That the delicate ear in its infancy

'May be dull'd, and the nostrils clos'd up,
'To teach mortal worms the path
'That leads from the gates of the Grave?'

Urizen heard them cry,
And his shudd'ring, waving wings
Went enormous above the red flames,
Drawing clouds of despair thro' the heavens
Of Europe as he went.
And his Books of brass, iron & gold
Melted over the land as he flew,
Heavy-waving, howling, weeping.

And he stood over Judea,
And stay'd in his ancient place,
And stretch'd his clouds over Jerusalem;

For Adam, a mouldering skeleton,
Lay bleach'd on the garden of Eden;
And Noah, as white as snow,
On the mountains of Ararat.

Then the thunders of Urizen bellow'd aloud
From his woven darkness above.

Orc, raging in European darkness,
Arose like a pillar of fire above the Alps,
Like a serpent of fiery flame!
    The sullen Earth
    Shrunk!

Forth from the dead dust, rattling bones to bones
Join: shaking convuls'd, the shiv'ring clay breathes,
And all flesh naked stands: Fathers and Friends,
Mothers & Infants, Kings & Warriors.

The Grave shrieks with delight & shakes
Her hollow womb & clasps the solid stem:
Her bosom swells with wild desire,

And milk & blood & glandous wine
In rivers rush & shout & dance,
On mountain, dale and plain.

The SONG of LOS is Ended.

Urizen Wept.

From VALA

OR

THE FOUR ZOAS

1797–1804

Night the Second

Rising upon his Couch of death Albion beheld his Sons.*
Turning his Eyes outward to Self, losing the Divine Vision,
Albion call'd Urizen & said: 'Behold these sick'ning
      Spheres,
'Whence is this voice of Enion that soundeth in my *Porches*?
'Take thou possession! take this Scepter! go forth in my
      might,
'For I am weary & must sleep in the dark sleep of Death.
'Thy brother Luvah hath smitten me, but pity thou his
      youth
'Tho' thou hast not piti'd my Age, O Urizen, Prince of
      Light.'

Urizen rose from the bright Feast like a star thro' the even-
      ing sky,
Exulting at the voice that call'd him from the Feast of envy.
First he beheld the body of Man, pale, cold; the horrors of
      death
Beneath his feet shot thro' him as he stood in the Human
      Brain,
And all its golden porches grew pale with his sickening
      light,
No more Exulting, for he saw Eternal Death beneath.

  * Words in italics are additions or corrections which Blake pencilled
in the MS.

Pale, he beheld futurity: pale, he beheld the Abyss
Where Enion, blind & age bent, wept in direful hunger
    craving,
All rav'ning like the hungry worm & like the silent grave.
Mighty was the draught of Voidness to draw Existence in.

Terrific Urizen strode above in fear & pale dismay.
He saw the indefinite space beneath & his soul shrunk with
    horror,
His feet upon the verge of Non Existence; his voice went
    forth:

Luvah & Vala trembling & shrinking beheld the great
    Work master
And heard his Word: 'Divide, ye bands, influence by in-
    fluence.
'Build we a Bower for heaven's darling in the grizly deep:
'*Build we the Mundane Shell around the Rock of Albion.*'

The Bands of Heaven flew thro' the air singing & shouting
    to Urizen.
Some fix'd the anvil, some the loom erected, some the plow
And harrow form'd & fram'd the harness of silver & ivory,
The golden compasses, the quadrant, & the rule & balance.
They erected the furnaces, they form'd the anvils of gold
    beaten in mills
Where winter beats incessant, fixing them firm on their base.
The bellows began to blow, & the Lions of Urizen stood
    round the anvil
And the leopards cover'd with skins of beasts tended the
    roaring fires,
Sublime, distinct, their lineaments divine of human beauty.
The tygers of wrath called the horses of instruction from
    their mangers,
They unloos'd them & put on the harness of gold & silver &
    ivory,

In human forms distinct they stood round Urizen, prince of
    Light,
Petrifying all the Human Imagination into rock & sand.
Groans ran along Tyburn's brook and along the River of
    Oxford
Among the Druid Temples. Albion groan'd on Tyburn's
    brook:
Albion gave his loud death groan. The Atlantic Mountains
    trembled.
Aloft the Moon fled with a cry: the Sun with streams of
    blood.
From Albion's Loins fled all Peoples and Nations of the
    Earth,
Fled with the noise of Slaughter, & the stars of heaven fled.
Jerusalem came down in a dire ruin over all the Earth,
She fell cold from Lambeth's Vales in groans & dewy
    death –
The dew of anxious souls, the death-sweat of the dying –
In every pillar'd hall & arched roof of Albion's skies.
The brother & the brother bathe in blood upon the Severn,
The Maiden weeping by. The father & the mother with
The Maiden's father & her mother fainting over the body,
And the Young Man, the Murderer, fleeing over the moun-
    tains.

Reuben slept on Penmaenmawr & Levi slept on Snowdon.
Their eyes, their ears, nostrils & tongues roll outward, they
    behold
What is within now seen without; they are raw to the hun-
    gry wind.
They become Natures far remote, in a little & dark Land.
The daughters of Albion girded around their garments of
    Needlework,
Stripping Jerusalem's curtains from mild demons of the
    hills;

Across Europe & Asia to China & Japan like lightnings
They go forth & return to Albion on his rocky couch:
Gwendolen, Ragan, Sabrina, Gonorill, Mehetabel, Cor-
della,
Boadicea, Conwenna, Estrild, Gwinefrid, Ignoge, Cambel,
Binding Jerusalem's Children in the dungeons of Babylon;
They play before the Armies, before the hounds of Nimrod,
While the Prince of Light on Salisbury plain among the
Druid Stones.

Rattling, the adamantine chains & hooks heave up the ore,
In mountainous masses plung'd in furnaces, & they shut &
seal'd
The furnaces a time & times; all the while blew the North
His cloudy bellows, & the South & East & dismal West,
And all the while the plow of iron cut the dreadful furrows
In Ulro, beneath Beulah, where the dead wail Night & Day.

Luvah was cast into the Furnaces of affliction & sealed,
And Vala fed in cruel delight the furnaces with fire.
Stern Urizen beheld, urg'd by necessity to keep
The evil day afar, & if perchance with iron power
He might avert his own despair; in woe & fear he saw
Vala incircle round the furnaces where Luvah was clos'd.
In joy she heard his howlings & forgot he was her Luvah,
With whom she walk'd in bliss in times of innocence &
youth.

Hear ye the voice of Luvah from the furnaces of Urizen:

'If I indeed am Vala's King, & ye, O sons of Men,
'The workmanship of Luvah's hands in times of Everlasting,
'When I call'd forth the Earth-worm from the cold & dark
obscure
'I nurtur'd her, I fed her with my rains & dews; she grew
'A scaled Serpent, yet I fed her tho' she hated me;
'Day after day she fed upon the mountains in Luvah's sight,
'I brought her thro' the Wilderness, a dry & thirsty land,

'And I commanded springs to rise for her in the black
　　desert,
'Till she became a Dragon, winged, bright & poisonous.
'I open'd all the floodgates of the heavens to quench her
　　thirst,
'And I commanded the Great deep to hide her in his hand
'Till she became a little weeping Infant a span long.
'I carried her in my bosom as a man carries a lamb,
'I loved her, I gave her all my soul & my delight,
'I hid her in soft gardens & in secret bowers of summer,
'Weaving mazes of delight along the sunny paradise,
'Inextricable labyrinths. She bore me sons & daughters,
'And they have taken her away & hid her from my sight.
'They have surrounded me with walls of iron & brass. O
　　Lamb
'Of God clothed in Luvah's garments! little knowest thou
'Of death Eternal, that we all go to Eternal Death,
'To our Primeval Chaos in fortuitous concourse of incoher-
　　ent
'Discordant principles of Love & Hate. I suffer affliction
'Because I love, for I was love, but hatred awakes in me,
'And Urizen, who was Faith & certainty, is chang'd to
　　Doubt;
'The hand of Urizen is upon me because I blotted out
'That Human delusion to deliver all the sons of God
'From bondage of the Human form. O first born Son of
　　Light,
'O Urizen my enemy, I weep for thy stern ambition,
'But weep in vain. O when will you return, Vala the Wan-
　　derer?'

These were the words of Luvah, patient in afflictions,
Reasoning from the loins in the unreal forms of Ulro's night.

And when Luvah, age after age, was quite melted with woe,
The fires of Vala faded like a shadow cold & pale,

An evanescent shadow; last she fell, a heap of Ashes
Beneath the furnaces, a woful heap in living death.

Then were the furnaces unseal'd with spades, & pickaxes
Roaring let out the fluid: the molten metal ran in channels
Cut by the plow of ages held in Urizen's strong hand
In many a valley, for the Bulls of Luvah drag'd the Plow.

With trembling horror pale, aghast the Children of Man
Stood on the infinite Earth & saw these visions in the air,
In waters & in earth beneath; they cried to one another,
'What are we terrors to one another? Come, O brethren,
        wherefore
'Was this wide Earth spread all abroad? not for wild beasts
        to roam.'
But many stood silent, & busied in their families.
And many said, 'We see no Visions in the darksom air.
'Measure the course of that sulphur orb that lights the dark-
        som day;
'Set stations on this breeding Earth & let us buy & sell.'
Others arose & schools erected, forming Instruments
To measure out the course of heaven. Stern Urizen beheld
In woe his brethren & his sons, in dark'ning woe lamenting
Upon the winds in clouds involv'd, Uttering his voice in
        thunders,
Commanding all the work with care & power & severity.

Then siez'd the Lions of Urizen their work, & heated in the
        forge
Roar the bright masses; thund'ring beat the hammers,
        many a pyramid
Is form'd & thrown down thund'ring into the deeps of Non
        Entity.
Heated red hot they, hizzing, rend their way down many a
        league
Till resting, each his basement finds; suspended there they
        stand

Casting their sparkles dire abroad into the dismal deep.
For, measur'd out in order'd spaces, the Sons of Urizen
With compasses divide the deep; they the strong scales erect
That Luvah rent from the faint Heart of the Fallen Man,
And weigh the massy Cubes, then fix them in their awful
    stations.

And all the time, in Caverns shut, the golden Looms erected
First spun, then wove the Atmospheres; there the Spider &
    Worm
Plied the wing'd shuttle, piping shrill thro' all the list'ning
    threads;
Beneath the Caverns roll the weights of lead & spindles of
    iron,
The enormous warp & woof rage direful in the affrighted
    deep.

While far into the vast unknown the strong wing'd Eagles
    bend
Their venturous flight in Human forms distinct; thro' dark-
    ness deep
They bear the woven draperies; on golden hooks they hang
    abroad
The universal curtains & spread out from Sun to Sun
The vehicles of light; they separate the furious particles
Into mild currents as the water mingles with the wine.

While thus the Spirits of strongest wing enlighten the dark
    deep,
The threads are spun & the cords twisted & drawn out; then
    the weak
Begin their work, & many a net is netted, many a net
Spread, & many a Spirit caught: innumerable the nets,
Innumerable the gins & traps, & many a soothing flute
Is form'd, & many a corded lyre outspread over the im-
    mense.

In cruel delight they trap the listeners, & in cruel delight
Bind them, condensing the strong energies into little com-
    pass
Some became seed of every plant that shall be planted;
    some
The bulbous roots, thrown up together into barns & garners.

Then rose the Builders. First the Architect divine his plan
Unfolds. The wondrous scaffold rear'd all round the infinite,
Quadrangular the building rose, the heavens squared by a
    line,
Trigons & cubes divide the elements in finite bonds.
Multitudes without number work incessant: the hewn stone
Is plac'd in beds of mortar mingled with the ashes of Vala.
Severe the labour; female slaves the mortar trod oppressed.

Twelve halls after the names of his twelve sons compos'd
The wondrous building, & three Central Domes after the
    Names
Of his three daughters were encompass'd by the twelve
    bright halls.
Every hall surrounded by bright Paradises of Delight
In which were towns & Cities, Nations, Seas, Mountains &
    Rivers.
Each Dome open'd toward four halls, & the Three Domes
    Encompass'd
The Golden Hall of Urizen, whose western side glow'd
    bright
With ever streaming fires beaming from his awful limbs.
His Shadowy Feminine Semblance here repos'd on a White
    Couch,
Or hover'd over his starry head; & when he smil'd she
    brighten'd
Like a bright Cloud in harvest; but when Urizen frown'd
    she wept
In mists over his carved throne; & when he turned his back

Upon his Golden hall & sought the Labyrinthine porches
Of his wide heaven, Trembling, cold, in paling fears she sat
A shadow of Despair; therefore toward the West, Urizen
    form'd
A recess in the wall for fires to glow upon the pale
Female's limbs in his absence, & her Daughters oft upon
A Golden Altar burnt perfumes: with Art Celestial form'd
Four square, sculptur'd & sweetly Engrav'd to please their
    shadowy mother.
Ascending into her misty garments the blue smoke roll'd to
    revive
Her cold limbs in the absence of her Lord. Also her sons,
With lives of Victims sacrificed upon an altar of brass
On the East side, Reviv'd her soul with lives of beasts &
    birds
Slain on the Altar, up ascending into her cloudy bosom.
Of terrible workmanship the Altar, labour of ten thousand
    Slaves,
One thousand Men of wondrous power spent their lives in
    its formation.
It stood on twelve steps nam'd after the names of her twelve
    sons,
And was Erected at the chief entrance of Urizen's hall.
When Urizen return'd from his immense labours & travels,
Descending she repos'd beside him, folding him around
In her bright skirts. Astonish'd & Confounded he beheld
Her shadowy form now separate; he shudder'd & was silent
Till her caresses & her tears reviv'd him to life & joy.
Two wills they had, two intellects, & not as in times of old.
This Urizen perciev'd, & silent brooded in dark'ning
    Clouds.
To him his Labour was but Sorrow & his Kingdom was
    Repentance.
He drave the Male Spirits all away from Ahania,
And she drave all the Females from him away.

Los joy'd, & Enitharmon laugh'd, saying, 'Let us go down
'And see this labour & sorrow.' They went down to see the
    woes
Of Vala & the woes of Luvah, to draw in their delights.

And Vala like a shadow oft appear'd to Urizen.

The King of Light beheld her mourning among the Brick
    kilns, compell'd
To labour night & day among the fires; her lamenting
    voice
Is heard when silent night returns & the labourers take their
    rest.

'O Lord, wilt thou not look upon our sore afflictions
'Among these flames incessant labouring? our hard masters
    laugh
'At all our sorrow. We are made to turn the wheel for water,
'To carry the heavy basket on our scorched shoulders, to
    sift
'The sand & ashes, & to mix the clay with tears & repent-
    ance.
'The times are now return'd upon us; we have given our-
    selves
'To scorn, and now are scorned by the slaves of our enemies.
'Our beauty is cover'd over with clay & ashes, & our backs
'Furrow'd with whips, & our flesh bruised with the heavy
    basket.
'Forgive us, O thou piteous one whom we have offended!
    forgive
'The weak remaining shadow of Vala that returns in sorrow
    to thee.

'*I see not Luvah as of old, I only see his feet*
'*Like pillars of fire travelling thro' darkness & non entity.*'

Thus she lamented day & night, compell'd to labour & sor-
    row.

Luvah in vain her lamentations heard: in vain his love
Brought him in various forms before her, still she knew him
    not,
Still she despis'd him, calling on his name & knowing him
    not,
Still hating, still professing love, still labouring in the smoke.

And Los & Enitharmon joy'd; they drank in tenfold joy
From all the sorrow of Luvah & the labour of Urizen.
And Enitharmon joy'd, Plotting to rend the secret cloud,
To plant divisions in the soul of Urizen & Ahania.

But infinitely beautiful the wondrous work arose
In sorrow and care, a Golden World whose porches round
    the heavens
And pillar'd halls & rooms reciev'd the eternal wandering
    stars.
A wondrous golden Building, many a window, many a
    door
And many a division let in & out the vast unknown.
Circled in infinite orb immoveable, within its walls & ceil-
    ings
The heavens were clos'd, and spirits mourn'd their bondage
    night & day,
And the Divine Vision appear'd in Luvah's robes of blood.

Thus was the Mundane shell builded by Urizen's strong Power.

Sorrowing went the Planters forth to plant, the Sowers to
    sow;
They dug the channels for the rivers, & they pour'd abroad
The seas & lakes; they rear'd the mountains & the rocks &
    hills
On broad pavilions, on pillar'd roofs & porches & high
    towers,
In beauteous order; thence arose soft clouds & exhalations
Wandering even to the sunny Cubes of light & heat,

For many a window ornamented with sweet ornaments
Look'd out into the World of Tharmas, where in ceaseless
    torrents
His billows roll, where monsters wander in the foamy paths.

On clouds the Sons of Urizen beheld Heaven walled round;
They weigh'd & order'd all, & Urizen comforted saw
The wondrous work flow forth like visible out of the invis-
    ible;
For the Divine Lamb, Even Jesus who is the Divine Vision
Permitted all, lest Man should fall into Eternal Death;
For when Luvah sunk down, himself put on the robes of
    blood
Lest the state call'd Luvah should cease; & the Divine Vis-
    ion
Walked in robes of blood till he who slept should awake.
Thus were the stars of heaven created like a golden chain
To bind the Body of Man to heaven from falling into the
    Abyss.
Each took his station & his course began with sorrow &
    care.

In sevens & tens & fifties, hundreds, thousands, number'd
    all
According to their various powers, subordinate to Urizen
And to his sons in their degrees & to his beauteous daugh-
    ters,
Travelling in silent majesty along their order'd ways
In right lined paths outmeasur'd by proportions of number,
    weight,
And measure, mathematic motion wondrous along the
    deep,
In fiery pyramid, or Cube, or unornamented pillar square
Of fire, far shining, travelling along even to its destin'd end;
Then falling down a terrible space, recovering in winter
    dire

Its wasted strength, it back returns upon a nether course,
Till fir'd with ardour fresh recruited in its humble season,
It rises up on high all summer, till its wearied course
Turns into autumn. Such the periods of many worlds.
Others triangular, right angled course maintain. Others
    obtuse,
Acute, Scalene, in simple paths; but others move
In intricate ways, biquadrate, Trapeziums, Rhombs,
    Rhomboids,
Paralellograms triple & quadruple, polygonic
In their amazing hard subdu'd course in the vast deep.

And Los & Enitharmon were drawn down by their desires,
Descending sweet upon the wind among soft harps &
    voices
To plant divisions in the Soul of Urizen & Ahania,
To conduct the Voice of Enion to Ahania's midnight pillow.

Urizen saw & envied, & his imagination was filled.
Repining he contemplated the past in his bright sphere,
Terrified with his heart & spirit at the visions of futurity
That his dread fancy form'd before him in the unform'd
    void.

For Los & Enitharmon walk'd forth on the dewy Earth
Contracting or expanding their all flexible senses
At will to murmur in the flowers small as the honey bee,
At will to stretch across the heavens & step from star to star,
Or standing on the Earth erect, or on the stormy waves
Driving the storms before them, or delighting in sunny
    beams,
While round their heads the Elemental Gods kept harmony.
And Los said: 'Lo, the Lilly pale & the rose redd'ning fierce
'Reproach thee, & the beamy gardens sicken at thy beauty;
'I grasp thy vest in my strong hands in vain, like water
    springs

144

'In the bright sands of Los evading my embrace; then I
     alone
'Wander among the virgins of the summer. Look, they cry,
'The poor forsaken Los, mock'd by the worm, the shelly
     snail,
'The Emmet & the beetle, hark! they laugh, & mock at
     Los.'

Enitharmon answer'd: 'Secure now from the smitings of thy
     Power, demon of fury,
'If the God enraptur'd me infold
'In clouds of sweet obscurity my beauteous form dissolving,
'Howl thou over the body of death; 'tis thine. But if among
     the virgins
'Of summer I have seen thee sleep & turn thy cheek de-
     lighted
'Upon the rose or lilly pale, or on a bank where sleep
'The beamy daughters of the light, starting, they rise, they
     flee
'From thy fierce love, for tho' I am dissolv'd in the bright
     God,
'My spirit still pursues thy false love over rocks & valleys.'

Los answer'd: 'Therefore fade I thus dissolv'd in raptur'd
     trance
'Thou canst repose on clouds of secrecy, while o'er my
     limbs
'Cold dews & hoary frost creep tho' I lie on banks of sum-
     mer
'Among the beauties of the World. Cold & repining Los
'Still dies for Enitharmon, nor a spirit springs from my dead
     corse;
'Then I am dead till thou revivest me with thy sweet song.
'Now taking on Ahania's form & now the form of Enion,
'I know thee not as once I knew thee in those blessed fields

'Where memory wishes to repose among the flocks of Thar-
     mas.'

Enitharmon answer'd: 'Wherefore didst thou throw thine
     arms around
'Ahania's Image? I deciev'd thee & will still decieve.
'Urizen saw thy sin & hid his beams in dark'ning clouds.
'I still keep watch altho' I tremble & wither across the
     heavens
'In strong vibrations of fierce jealousy; for thou art mine,
'Created for my will, my slave, tho' strong, tho' I am weak.
'Farewell, the God calls me away. I depart in my sweet
     bliss.'

She fled, vanishing on the wind, And left a dead cold corse
In Los's arms; howlings began over the body of death.
Los spoke. 'Thy God in vain shall call thee if by my strong
     power
'I can infuse my dear revenge into his glowing breast.
'Then jealousy shall shadow all his mountains & Ahania
'Curse thee, thou plague of woful Los, & seek revenge on
     thee.'

So saying in deep sobs he languish'd till dead he also fell.
Night passed, & Enitharmon, e'er the dawn, return'd in
     bliss.
She sang O'er Los reviving him to Life: his groans were
     terrible;
But thus she sang:
  'I sieze the sphery harp, I strike the strings.

  'At the first sound the Golden sun arises from the deep
  'And shakes his awful hair,
  'The Eccho wakes the moon to unbind her silver locks,
  'The golden sun bears on my song
  'And nine bright spheres of harmony rise round the fiery
        king.

'The joy of woman is the death of her most best beloved
'Who dies for Love of her
'In torments of fierce jealousy & pangs of adoration.
'The Lovers' night bears on my song
'And the nine spheres rejoice beneath my powerful con-
     troll.

'They sing unceasing to the notes of my immortal hand.
'The solemn, silent moon
'Reverberates the living harmony upon my limbs,
'The birds & beasts rejoice & play,
'And every one seeks for his mate to prove his inmost joy.

'Furious & terrible they sport & red the nether deep;
'The deep lifts up his rugged head,
'And lost in infinite humming wings vanishes with a cry.
'The fading cry is ever dying,
'The living voice is ever living in its inmost joy.

'Arise, you little glancing wings & sing your infant joy!
'Arise & drink your bliss!
'For every thing that lives is holy; for the source of life
'Descends to be a weeping babe;
'For the Earthworm renews the moisture of the sandy
     plain.
'Now my left hand I stretch to earth beneath,
'And strike the terrible string.
'I wake sweet joy in dens of sorrow & I plant a smile
'In forests of affliction,
'And wake the bubbling springs of life in regions of dark
     death.

'O I am weary! lay thine hand upon me or I faint,
'I faint beneath these beams of thine,
'For thou hast touch'd my five senses & they answer'd
     thee.

'Now I am nothing, & I sink
'And on the bed of silence sleep till thou awakest me.'

Thus sang the Lovely one in Rapturous delusive trance.
Los heard, reviving; he siez'd her in his arms; delusive
    hopes
Kindling, she led him into shadows & thence fled out-
    stretch'd
Upon the immense like a bright rainbow, weeping & smil-
    ing & fading.

Thus liv'd Los, driving Enion far into the *deathful* infinite
That he may also draw Ahania's spirit into her Vortex.
Ah, happy blindness! Enion sees not the terrors of the un-
    certain,
And thus she wails from the dark deep; the golden heavens
    tremble:

'I am made to sow the thistle for wheat, the nettle for a
    nourishing dainty.
'I have planted a false oath in the earth; it has brought
    forth a poison tree.
'I have chosen the serpent for a councellor, & the dog
'For a schoolmaster to my children.
'I have blotted out from light & living the dove & night-
    ingale,
'And I have caused the earth worm to beg from door to
    door.

'I have taught the thief a secret path into the house of the
    just.
'I have taught pale artifice to spread his nets upon the
    morning.
'My heavens are brass, my earth is iron, my moon a clod of
    clay,
'My sun a pestilence burning at noon & a vapour of death
    in night.

'What is the price of Experience? do men buy it for a song?
'Or wisdom for a dance in the street? No, it is bought with
      the price
'Of all that a man hath, his house, his wife, his children.
'Wisdom is sold in the desolate market where none come to
      buy,
'And in the wither'd field where the farmer plows for bread
      in vain.

'It is an easy thing to triumph in the summer's sun
'And in the vintage & to sing on the waggon loaded with
      corn.
'It is an easy thing to talk of patience to the afflicted,
'To speak the laws of prudence to the homeless wanderer,
'To listen to the hungry raven's cry in wintry season
'When the red blood is fill'd with wine & with the marrow
      of lambs.

'It is an easy thing to laugh at wrathful elements,
'To hear the dog howl at the wintry door, the ox in the
      slaughter house moan;
'To see a god on every wind & a blessing on every blast;
'To hear sounds of love in the thunder storm that destroys
      our enemies' house;
'To rejoice in the blight that covers his field, & the sickness
      that cuts off his children,
'While our olive & vine sing & laugh round our door, & our
      children bring fruits & flowers.

'Then the groan & the dolor are quite forgotten, & the
      slave grinding at the mill,
'And the captive in chains, & the poor in the prison, & the
      soldier in the field
'When the shatter'd bone hath laid him groaning among the
      happier dead.

'It is an easy thing to rejoice in the tents of prosperity:
'Thus could I sing & thus rejoice: but it is not so with me.'

Ahania heard the Lamentation, & a swift Vibration
Spread thro' her Golden frame. She rose up e'er the dawn
     of day
When Urizen slept on his couch: drawn thro' unbounded
     space
On the margin of Non Entity the bright Female came.
There she beheld the *Spectrous* form of Enion in the Void,
And never from that moment could she rest upon her pillow.

END OF THE SECOND NIGHT

VALA

Night the Third

Now sat the King of Light on high upon his starry throne,
And bright Ahania bow'd herself before his splendid feet.

'O Urizen, look on *Me*; like a mournful stream
'*I* Embrace round thy knees & wet *My* bright hair with *My*
    tears.
'Why sighs my Lord? are not the morning stars thy obedient
    Sons?
'Do they not bow their bright heads at thy voice? at thy
    command
'Do they not fly into their stations & return their light to
    thee?
'The immortal Atmospheres are thine; there thou art seen
    in glory
'Surrounded by the ever changing Daughters of the Light.
'Why wilt thou look upon futurity, dark'ning present joy?'

She ceas'd; the Prince his light obscur'd & the splendors of
    his crown
Infolded in thick clouds from whence his mighty voice burst
    forth:

'O bright Ahania, a Boy is born of the dark Ocean
'Whom Urizen doth serve, with Light replenishing his dark-
    ness.
'I am set here a King of trouble, commanded here to serve
'And do my ministry to those who eat of my wide table.
'All this is mine, yet I must serve, & that Prophetic boy
'Must grow up to command his Prince; *but hear my determin'd
    decree*:
'Vala shall become a Worm in Enitharmon's Womb,

'Laying her seed upon the fibres, soon to issue forth,
'And Luvah in the loins of Los a dark & furious death.
'Alas for me! what will become of me at that dread time?'

Ahania bow'd her head & wept seven days before the King;
And on the eighth day, when his clouds unfolded from his
    throne,
She rais'd her bright head sweet perfum'd & thus with
    heavenly voice:

'O Prince, the Eternal One hath set thee leader of his hosts,
'Raise then thy radiant eyes to him, raise thy obedient
    hands,
'And comforts shall descend from heaven into thy dark'ning
    clouds.
'Leave all futurity to him. Resume thy fields of Light.
'Why didst thou listen to the voice of Luvah that dread
    morn
'To give the immortal steeds of light to his deceitful hands?
'No longer now obedient to thy will, thou art compell'd
'To forge the curbs of iron & brass, to build the iron man-
    gers,
'To feed them with intoxication from the wine presses of
    Luvah
'Till the Divine Vision & Fruition is quite obliterated.
'They call thy lions to the field of blood; they rouze thy
    tygers
'Out of the halls of justice, till these dens thy wisdom fram'd
'Golden & beautiful, but O how unlike those sweet fields
    of bliss
'Where liberty was justice, & eternal science was mercy.
'Then, O my dear lord, listen to Ahania, listen to the vision,
'The vision of Ahania in the slumbers of Urizen
'When Urizen slept in the porch & the Ancient Man was
    smitten.

'The Dark'ning Man walk'd on the steps of fire before his
    halls,
'And Vala walk'd with him in dreams of soft deluding
    slumber.
'He looked up & saw thee, Prince of Light, thy splendor
    faded,
'But saw not Los nor Enitharmon for Luvah hid them in
    shadow
'*In* a soft cloud outstretch'd across, & Luvah dwelt in the
    cloud.

'Then Man ascended mourning into the splendors of his
    palace,
'Above him rose a Shadow from his wearied intellect
'Of living gold, pure, perfect, holy; in white linen pure he
    hover'd,
'A sweet entrancing self delusion, a wat'ry vision of Man
'Soft exulting in existence, all the Man absorbing.

'Man fell upon his face prostrate before the wat'ry shadow,
'Saying, "O Lord, whence is this change? thou knowest I
    am nothing."
'And Vala trembled & cover'd her face, & her locks were
    spread on the pavement.
'*We* heard astonish'd at the Vision, & *our* hearts trembled
    within *us*.
'*We* heard the voice of the Slumberous Man, & thus he
    spoke
'Idolatrous to his own Shadow, words of Eternity uttering:
'"O I am nothing when I enter into judgment with thee.
'"If thou withdraw thy breath I die & vanish into Hades;
'"If thou dost lay thine hand upon me, behold I am silent;
'"If thou withhold thine hand I perish like a fallen leaf.
'"O I am nothing, & to nothing must return again.
'"If thou withdraw thy breath, behold I am oblivion."

'He ceas'd: the shadowy voice was silent, but the cloud
    hover'd over their heads
'In golden wreathes, the sorrow of Man, & the balmy drops
    fell down,
'And Lo, that Son of Man, that shadowy Spirit of *Albion*,
'Luvah, descended from the cloud. In terror *Albion* rose:
'Indignant rose the Awful Man & turn'd his back on Vala.

'We heard the Voice of Albion starting from his sleep:
'"Why roll thy clouds in sick'ning mists? I can no longer
    hide
'"The dismal vision of mine eyes. O love & life & light!
'"Prophetic dreads urge me to speak: futurity is before me
'"Like a dark lamp. Eternal death haunts all my expecta-
    tion.
'"Rent from Eternal Brotherhood we die & are no more.

'"Whence is this voice crying, Enion! that soundeth in my
    ears?
'"O cruel pity! O dark deceit! can Love seek for domin-
    ion?"

'And Luvah strove to gain dominion over *mighty Albion*.
'They strove together above the Body where Vala was in-
    clos'd
'And the dark Body of *Albion* left prostrate upon the crystal
    pavement,
'Cover'd with boils from head to foot, the terrible smitings
    of Luvah.

'Then frown'd *Albion* & put forth Luvah from his presence
'(I heard him: frown not, Urizen, but listen to my Vision)
'Saying, "Go & die the Death of Man for Vala the sweet
    wanderer.
'"I will turn the volutions of your Ears outward, & bend
    your Nostrils

'"Downward, & your fluxile Eyes englob'd roll round in
      fear;

'"Your with'ring Lips & Tongue shrink up into a narrow
      circle

'"Till into narrow forms you creep. Go take your fiery way

'"And learn what 'tis to absorb the Man, you Spirits of
      Pity & Love."

'O Urizen, why art thou pale at the visions of Ahania?

'Listen to her who loves thee, lest we also are driven away.

'They heard the Voice & fled, swift as the winter's setting
      sun.

'And now the Human Blood foam'd high. I saw that Luvah
      & Vala

'Went down the Human Heart, where Paradise & its joys
      abounded,

'In jealous fears, in fury & rage, & flames roll'd round their
      fervid feet,

'And the vast form of Nature like a Serpent play'd before
      them;

'And as they went, in folding fires & thunders of the deep,

'Vala shrunk in like the dark sea that leaves its slimy banks,

'And from her bosom Luvah fell far as the east & west

'And the vast form of Nature, like a Serpent, roll'd between.

'*Whether this is Jerusalem or Babylon we know not.*

'*All is Confusion. All is tumult, & we alone are escaped.*'

She ended, for his wrathful throne burst forth the black hail
      storm.

(Albion clos'd the Western Gate, & shut America out by
      the Atlantic, for a curse, and hidden horror, and an
      altar of victims to Sin and Repentance.)

'Am I not God?' said Urizen. 'Who is Equal to me?

'Do I not stretch the heavens abroad, or fold them up like a
      garment?'

He spoke, mustering his heavy clouds around him, black,
    opake.

Then thunders roll'd around & lightnings darted to and fro;

His visage chang'd to darkness, & his strong right hand
    came forth

To cast Ahania to the Earth; he siez'd her by the hair

And threw her from the steps of ice that froze around his
    throne,

Saying, 'Art thou also become like Vala? thus I cast thee
    out!

'Shall the feminine indolent bliss, the indulgent self of weari-
    ness,

'The passive idle sleep, the enormous night & darkness of
    Death

'Set herself up to give her laws to the active masculine
    virtue?

'Thou little diminutive portion that dar'st be a counterpart,

'Thy passivity, thy laws of obedience & insincerity

'Are my abhorrence. Wherefore hast thou taken that fair
    form?

'Whence is this power given to thee? Once thou wast in my
    breast

'A sluggish current of dim waters on whose verdant margin

'A cavern shagg'd with horrid shades, dark, cool & deadly,
    where

'I laid my head in the hot noon after the broken clods

'Had wearied me; there I laid my plow, & there my horses
    fed:

'And thou hast risen with thy moist locks into a wat'ry
    image

'Reflecting all my indolence, my weakness & my death,

'To weigh me down beneath the grave into non Entity

'Where Luvah strives, scorned by Vala, age after age wand-
    ering,

'Shrinking & shrinking from her Lord & calling him the
      Tempter.
'And art thou also become like Vala? thus I cast thee out!'

So loud in thunders spoke the King, folded in dark despair,
And threw Ahania from his bosom obdurate. She fell like
      lightning.
Then fled the sons of Urizen from his thunderous throne
      petrific;
They fled to East & West &˙left the North & South of
      Heaven.
A crash ran thro' the immense. The bounds of Destiny were
      broken.
The bounds of Destiny crash'd direful, & the swelling sea
Burst from its bonds in whirlpools fierce, roaring with
      Human voice,
Triumphing even to the stars at bright Ahania's fall.

Down from the dismal North the Prince in thunders & thick
      clouds –
As when the thunderbolt down falleth on the appointed
      place –
Fell down, down rushing, ruining, thundering, shuddering,
Into the Caverns of the Grave & places of Human Seed
Where the impressions of Despair & Hope enroot for ever:
A world of Darkness. Ahania fell far into Non Entity.

She Continued falling. Loud the Crash continu'd, loud &
      Hoarse.
From the Crash roared a flame of blue sulphureous fire,
      from the flame
A dolorous groan that struck with dumbness all confusion,
Swallowing up the horrible din in agony on agony.
Thro' the Confusion, like a crack across from immense to
      immense,
Loud, strong, a universal groan of death, louder

Than all the wracking elements, deafen'd & rended worse

Than Urizen & all his hosts in curst despair down rushing.

But from the Dolorous Groan one like a shadow of smoke
    appear'd,

And human bones rattling together in the smoke & stamp-
    ing

The nether Abyss, & gnashing in fierce despair, panting in
    sobs,

Thick, short, incessant, bursting, sobbing, deep despairing,
    stamping, struggling,

Struggling to utter the voice of Man, struggling to take the
    features of Man, struggling

To take the limbs of Man, at length emerging from the
    smoke

Of Urizen dashed in pieces from his precipitant fall,

Tharmas rear'd up his hands & stood on the affrighted
    Ocean:

The dead rear'd up his Voice & stood on the resounding
    shore,

Crying: 'Fury in my limbs! destruction in my bones &
    marrow!

'My skull riven into filaments, my eyes into sea jellies

'Floating upon the tide wander bubbling & bubbling,

'Uttering my lamentations & begetting little monsters

'Who sit mocking upon the little pebbles of the tide

'In all my rivers & on dried shells that the fish

'Have quite forsaken. O fool! fool! to lose my sweetest bliss.

'Where art thou, Enion? ah, too near to cunning, too far off

'And yet too near. Dash'd down I send thee into distant
    darkness

'Far as my strength can hurl thee; wander there & laugh &
    play

'Among the frozen arrows; they will tear thy tender flesh.

'Fall off afar from Tharmas, come not too near my strong
    fury.

'Scream & fall off & laugh at Tharmas, lovely summer
    beauty,
'Till winter rends thee into Shivers as thou hast rended me.'

So Tharmas bellow'd o'er the ocean, thund'ring, sobbing,
    bursting.
The bounds of Destiny were broken, & hatred now began
Instead of love to Enion. Enion, blind & age bent,
Plung'd into the cold billows, living a life in midst of waters;
In terrors she wither'd away to Entuthon Benithon,
A world of deep darkness where all things in horrors are
    rooted.

These are the words of Enion, heard from the cold waves of
    despair:
'O Tharmas, I had lost thee, & when I hoped I had found
    thee,
'O Tharmas, do not thou destroy me quite, but let
'A little shadow, but a little showery form of Enion
'Be near thee, loved Terror; let me still remain, & then do
    thou
'Thy righteous doom upon me; only let me hear thy voice.
'Driven by thy rage I wander like a cloud into the deep
'Where never yet Existence came; there losing all my life
'I back return weaker & weaker; consume me not away
'In thy great wrath; tho' I have sinned, tho' I have re-
    bell'd
'Make me not like the things forgotten as they had not been.
'Make not the thing that loveth thee a tear wiped
    away.'

Tharmas replied, riding on storms, his voice of Thunder
    roll'd:
'Image of grief, thy fading lineaments make my eyelids fail.
'What have I done? both rage & mercy are alike to me;
'Looking upon thee, Image of faint waters, I recoil

'From my fierce rage into thy semblance. Enion, return.
'Why does thy piteous face Evanish like a rainy cloud
'Melting, a shower of falling tears, nothing but tears!
    Enion,
'Substanceless, voiceless, weeping, vanish'd, nothing but
    tears! Enion,
'Art thou for ever vanish'd from the wat'ry eyes of Thar-
    mas?
'Rage, Rage shall never from my bosom: winds & waters of
    woe
'Consuming all, to the end consuming. Love and Hope are
    ended.'

For now no more remain'd of Enion in the dismal air,
Only a voice eternal wailing in the Elements.

Where Enion, blind & age bent, wander'd, Ahania wanders
    now:
She wanders in Eternal fear of falling into the indefinite,
For her bright eyes behold the Abyss. Sometimes a little
    sleep
Weighs down her eyelids; then she falls; then starting,
    wakes in fears
Sleepless to wander round, repell'd on the margin of Non
    Entity.

THE END OF THE THIRD NIGHT

MILTON

A POEM IN TWO BOOKS

To Justify the Ways of God to Men

Written and etched 1804–1808

Preface

The Stolen and Perverted Writings of Homer & Ovid, of Plato & Cicero, which all Men ought to contemn, are set up by artifice against the Sublime of the Bible; but when the New Age is at leisure to Pronounce, all will be set right, & those Grand Works of the more ancient & consciously & professedly Inspired Men will hold their proper rank, & the Daughters of Memory shall become the Daughters of Inspiration. Shakespeare & Milton were both curb'd by the general malady & infection from the silly Greek & Latin slaves of the Sword.

Rouze up, O Young Men of the New Age! set your foreheads against the ignorant Hirelings! For we have Hirelings in the Camp, the Court & the University, who would, if they could, for ever depress Mental & prolong Corporeal War. Painters! on you I call. Sculptors! Architects! Suffer not the fashonable Fools to depress your powers by the prices they pretend to give for contemptible works, or the expensive advertizing boasts that they make of such works; believe Christ & his Apostles that there is a Class of Men whose whole delight is in Destroying. We do not want either Greek or Roman Models if we are but just & true to our own Imaginations, those Worlds of Eternity in which we shall live for ever in Jesus our Lord.

And did those feet in ancient time
Walk upon England's mountains green?
And was the holy Lamb of God
On England's pleasant pastures seen?

And did the Countenance Divine
Shine forth upon our clouded hills?
And was Jerusalem builded here
Among these dark Satanic Mills?

Bring me my Bow of burning gold:
Bring me my Arrows of desire:
Bring me my Spear: O clouds unfold!
Bring me my Chariot of fire.

I will not cease from Mental Fight,
Nor shall my Sword sleep in my hand
Till we have built Jerusalem
In England's green & pleasant Land.

'Would to God that all the Lord's people were Prophets.'

NUMBERS, xi ch., 29 v.

From MILTON: *Book the First*

Then the Divine Family said: 'Six Thousand Years are now
'Accomplish'd in this World of Sorrow. Milton's Angel
    knew
'The Universal Dictate, and you also feel this Dictate.
'And now you know this World of Sorrow and feel Pity.
    Obey
'The Dictate! Watch over this World, and with your brood-
    ing wings
'Renew it to Eternal Life. Lo! I am with you alway.
'But you cannot renew Milton: he goes to Eternal Death.'

So spake the Family Divine as One Man, even Jesus,
Uniting in One with Ololon, & the appearance of One
    Man,
Jesus the Saviour, appear'd coming in the Clouds of Ololon.

24

Tho' driven away with the Seven Starry Ones into the
    Ulro,
Yet the Divine Vision remains Every-where For-ever. Amen.
And Ololon lamented for Milton with a great lamentation.

While Los heard indistinct in fear, what time I bound my
    sandals
On to walk forward thro' Eternity, Los descended to me:
And Los behind me stood, a terrible flaming Sun, just close
Behind my back. I turned round in terror, and behold!
Los stood in that fierce glowing fire, & he also stoop'd down
And bound my sandals on in Udan-Adan; trembling I
    stood
Exceedingly with fear & terror, standing in the Vale

Of Lambeth; but he kissed me and wish'd me health,
And I became One Man with him arising in my strength.
'Twas too late now to recede. Los had enter'd into my soul:
His terrors now possess'd me whole! I arose in fury &
    strength.

'I am that Shadowy Prophet who Six Thousand Years ago
'Fell from my station in the Eternal bosom. Six Thousand
    Years
'Are finish'd. I return! both Time & Space obey my will.
'I in Six Thousand Years walk up and down; for not one
    Moment
'Of Time is lost, nor one Event of Space unpermanent,
'But all remain: every fabric of Six Thousand Years
'Remains permanent, tho' on the Earth where Satan
'Fell and was cut off, all things vanish & are seen no more,
'They vanish not from me & mine, we guard them first &
    last.
'The generations of men run on in the tide of Time,
'But leave their destin'd lineaments permanent for ever &
    ever.'

So spoke Los as we went along to his supreme abode.

Rintrah and Palamabron met us at the Gate of Golgonooza,
Clouded with discontent & brooding in their minds terrible
    things.

They said: 'O Father most beloved! O merciful Parent
'Pitying and permitting evil, tho' strong & mighty to
    destroy!
'Whence is this Shadow terrible? wherefore dost thou
    refuse
'To throw him into the Furnaces? knowest thou not that he
'Will unchain Orc & let loose Satan, Og, Sihon & Anak
'Upon the Body of Albion? for this he is come! behold it
    written

'Upon his fibrous left Foot black, most dismal to our eyes.

'The Shadowy Female shudders thro' heaven in torment inexpressible,

'And all the Daughters of Los prophetic wail; yet in deceit

'They weave a new Religion from new Jealousy of Theotormon.

'Milton's Religion is the cause: there is no end to destruction.

'Seeing the Churches at their Period in terror & despair,

'Rahab created Voltaire, Tirzah created Rousseau,

'Asserting the Self-righteousness against the Universal Saviour,

'Mocking the Confessors & Martyrs, claiming Self-righteousness,

'With cruel Virtue making War upon the Lamb's Redeemed

'To perpetuate War & Glory, to perpetuate the Laws of Sin.

'They perverted Swedenborg's Visions in Beulah & in Ulro

'To destroy Jerusalem as a Harlot & her Sons as Reprobates,

'To raise up Mystery the Virgin Harlot, Mother of War,

'Babylon the Great, the Abominations of Desolation.

'O Swedenborg! strongest of men, the Samson shorn by the Churches,

'Shewing the Transgressors in Hell, the proud Warriors in Heaven,

'Heaven as a Punisher, & Hell as One under Punishment,

'With Laws from Plato & his Greeks to renew the Trojan Gods

'In Albion, & to deny the value of the Saviour's blood.

'But then I rais'd up Whitefield, Palamabron rais'd up Westley,

'And these are the cries of the Churches before the two Witnesses.

'Faith in God, the dear Saviour who took on the likeness of
    men,
'Becoming obedient to death, even the death of the Cross.
'The Witnesses lie dead in the Street of the Great City:
'No Faith is in all the Earth: the Book of God is trodden
    under Foot.
'He sent his two Servants, Whitefield & Westley: were they
    Prophets,
'Or were they Idiots or Madmen? shew us Miracles!

25

'Can you have greater Miracles than these? Men who
    devote
'Their life's whole comfort to intire scorn & injury & death?
'Awake, thou sleeper on the Rock of Eternity! Albion
    awake!
'The trumpet of Judgment hath twice sounded: all Nations
    are awake,
'But thou art still heavy and dull. Awake, Albion awake!
'Lo, Orc arises on the Atlantic. Lo, his blood and fire
'Glow on America's shore. Albion turns upon his Couch:
'He listens to the sounds of War, astonished and confoun-
    ded:
'He weeps into the Atlantic deep, yet still in dismal dreams
'Unwaken'd, and the Covering Cherub advances from the
    East.
'How long shall we lay dead in the Street of the great City?
'How long beneath the Covering Cherub give our Emana-
    tions?
'Milton will utterly consume us & thee our beloved Father.
'He hath enter'd into the Covering Cherub, becoming one
    with
'Albion's dread Sons: Hand, Hyle & Coban surround him
    as

'A girdle, Gwendolen & Conwenna as a garment woven
'Of War & Religion; let us descend & bring him chained
'To Bowlahoola, O father most beloved! O mild Parent!
'Cruel in thy mildness, pitying and permitting evil,
'Tho' strong and mighty to destroy, O Los our beloved
  Father!'

Like the black storm, coming out of Chaos beyond the stars,
It issues thro' the dark & intricate caves of the Mundane
  Shell,
Passing the planetary visions & the well adorned Firma-
  ment.
The Sun rolls into Chaos & the stars into the Desarts,
And then the storms become visible, audible & terrible,
Covering the light of day & rolling down upon the moun-
  tains,
Deluge all the country round. Such is a vision of Los
When Rintrah & Palamabron spake, and such his stormy
  face
Appear'd as does the face of heaven when cover'd with
  thick storms,
Pitying and loving tho' in frowns of terrible perturbation.

But Los dispers'd the clouds even as the strong winds of
  Jehovah,
And Los thus spoke: 'O noble Sons, be patient yet a little!
'I have embrac'd the falling Death, he is become One with
  me:
'O Sons, we live not by wrath, by mercy alone we live!
'I recollect an old Prophecy in Eden recorded in gold and
  oft
'Sung to the harp, That Milton of the land of Albion
'Should up ascend forward from Felpham's Vale & break
  the Chain
'Of Jealousy from all its roots; be patient therefore, O my
  Sons!

'These lovely Females form sweet night and silence and
    secret
'Obscurities to hide from Satan's Watch-Fiends Human
    loves
'And graces, lest they write them in their Books & in the
    Scroll
'Of mortal life to condemn the accused, who at Satan's Bar
'Tremble in Spectrous Bodies continually day and night,
'While on the Earth they live in sorrowful Vegetations.
'O when shall we tread our Wine-presses in heaven and
    Reap
'Our wheat with shoutings of joy, and leave the Earth in
    peace?
'Remember how Calvin and Luther in fury premature
'Sow'd War and stern division between Papists & Protest-
    ants.
'Let it not be so now! O go not forth in Martyrdoms &
    Wars!
'We were plac'd here by the Universal Brotherhood &
    Mercy
'With powers fitted to circumscribe this dark Satanic death,
'And that the Seven Eyes of God may have space for Re-
    demption.
'But how this is as yet we know not, and we cannot know
'Till Albion is arisen; then patient wait a little while.
'Six Thousand years are pass'd away, the end approaches
    fast:
'This mighty one is come from Eden, he is of the Elect
'Who died from Earth & he is return'd before the Judgment.
    This thing
'Was never known, that one of the holy dead should willing
    return.
'Then patient wait a little while till the Last Vintage is over,
'Till we have quench'd the Sun of Salah in the Lake of
    Udan-Adan.

'O my dear Sons, leave not your Father as your brethren
  left me!
'Twelve Sons successive fled away in that thousand years of
  sorrow

26

'Of Palamabron's Harrow & of Rintrah's wrath & fury:
'Reuben & Manazzoth & Gad & Simeon & Levi
'And Ephraim & Judah were Generated because
'They left me, wandering with Tirzah. Enitharmon wept
'One thousand years, and all the Earth was in a wat'ry
  deluge.
'We call'd him Menassheh because of the Generations of
  Tirzah,
'Because of Satan: & the Seven Eyes of God continually
'Guard round them, but I, the Fourth Zoa, am also set
'The Watchman of Eternity: the Three are not, & I am
  preserved.
'Still my four mighty ones are left to me in Golgonooza,
'Still Rintrah fierce, and Palamabron mild & piteous,
'Theotormon fill'd with care, Bromion loving Science.
'You, O my Sons, still guard round Los: O wander not &
  leave me!
'Rintrah, thou well rememberest when Amalek & Canaan
'Fled with their Sister Moab into that abhorred Void,
'They became Nations in our sight beneath the hands of
  Tirzah.
'And Palamabron, thou rememberest when Joseph, an in-
  fant,
'Stolen from his nurse's cradle, wrap'd in needle-work
'Of emblematic texture, was sold to the Amalekite
'Who carried him down into Egypt where Ephraim & Me-
  nassheh
'Gather'd my Sons together in the Sands of Midian.

'And if you also flee away and leave your Father's side
'Following Milton into Ulro, altho' your power is great,
'Surely you also shall become poor mortal vegetations
'Beneath the Moon of Ulro: pity then your Father's tears.
'When Jesus rais'd Lazarus from the Grave I stood & saw
'Lazarus, who is the Vehicular Body of Albion the Re-
        deem'd,
'Arise into the Covering Cherub, who is the Spectre of
        Albion,
'By martyrdoms to suffer, to watch over the Sleeping Body
'Upon his Rock beneath his Tomb. I saw the Covering
        Cherub
'Divide Four-fold into Four Churches when Lazarus arose,
'Paul, Constantine, Charlemaine, Luther; behold, they
        stand before us
'Stretch'd over Europe & Asia! come O Sons, come, come
        away!

'Arise, O Sons, give all your strength against Eternal Death,
'Lest we are vegetated, for Cathedron's Looms weave only
        Death,
'A Web of Death: & were it not for Bowlahoola & Alla-
        manda
'No Human Form but only a Fibrous Vegetation,
'A Polypus of soft affections without Thought or Vision,
'Must tremble in the Heavens & Earths thro' all the Ulro
        space.
'Throw all the Vegetated Mortals into Bowlahoola:
'But as to this Elected Form who is return'd again,
'He is the Signal that the Last Vintage now approaches,
'No Vegetation may go on till all the Earth is reap'd.'

So Los spoke. Furious they descended to Bowlahoola &
        Allamanda,
Indignant, unconvinc'd by Los's arguments & thunders
        rolling:

They saw that wrath now sway'd and now pity absorb'd
      him.
As it was so it remain'd & no hope of an end.
Bowlahoola is nam'd Law by mortals; Tharmas founded it,
Because of Satan, before Luban in the City of Golgonooza.
But Golgonooza is nam'd Art & Manufacture by mortal
      men.

In Bowlahoola Los's Anvils stand & his Furnaces rage;
Thundering the Hammers beat & the Bellows blow loud,
Living, self moving, mourning, lamenting & howling in-
      cessantly.
Bowlahoola thro' all its porches feels, tho' too fast founded
Its pillars & porticoes to tremble at the force
Of mortal or immortal arm: and softly lilling flutes,
Accordant with the horrid labours, make sweet melody.
The Bellows are the Animal Lungs: the Hammers the Ani-
      mal Heart:
The Furnaces the Stomach for digestion: terrible their fury.
Thousands & thousands labour, thousands play on instru-
      ments
Stringed or fluted to ameliorate the sorrows of slavery.
Loud sport the dancers in the dance of death, rejoicing in
      carnage.
The hard dentant Hammers are lull'd by the flutes' lula lula,
The bellowing Furnaces blare by the long sounding clarion,
The double drum drowns howls & groans, the shrill fife
      shrieks & cries,
The crooked horn mellows the hoarse raving serpent, ter-
      rible but harmonious:
Bowlahoola is the Stomach in every individual man.
Los is by mortals nam'd Time, Enitharmon is nam'd Space:
But they depict him bald & aged who is in eternal youth
All powerful and his locks flourish like the brows of morn-
      ing:

He is the Spirit of Prophecy, the ever apparent Elias.
Time is the mercy of Eternity; without Time's swiftness,
Which is the swiftest of all things, all were eternal torment.
All the Gods of the Kingdoms of Earth labour in Los's
    Halls:
Every one is a fallen Son of the Spirit of Prophecy.
He is the Fourth Zoa that stood around the Throne Divine.

27

Loud shout the Sons of Luvah at the Wine-presses as Los
    descended
With Rintrah & Palamabron in his fires of resistless fury.

The Wine-press on the Rhine groans loud, but all its central
    beams
Act more terrific in the central Cities of the Nations
Where Human Thought is crush'd beneath the iron hand of
    Power:
There Los puts all into the Press, the Opressor & the
    Opressed
Together, ripe for the Harvest & Vintage & ready for the
    Loom.

They sang at the Vintage: 'This is the Last Vintage, &
    Seed
'Shall no more be sown upon Earth till all the Vintage is
    over
'And all gather'd in, till the Plow has pass'd over the Na-
    tions
'And the Harrow & heavy thundering Roller upon the
    mountains.'

And loud the Souls howl round the Porches of Golgonooza,
Crying: 'O God deliver us to the Heavens or to the Earths,

'That we may preach righteousness & punish the sinner
    with death.'
But Los refused, till all the Vintage of Earth was gathered
    in.
And Los stood & cried to the Labourers of the Vintage in
    voice of awe:

'Fellow Labourers! The Great Vintage & Harvest is now
    upon Earth.
'The whole extent of the Globe is explored. Every scatter'd
    Atom
'Of Human Intellect now is flocking to the sound of the
    Trumpet.
'All the Wisdom which was hidden in caves & dens from
    ancient
'Time is now sought out from Animal & Vegetable &
    Mineral.
'The Awakener is come outstretch'd over Europe: the Vis-
    ion of God is fulfilled:
'The Ancient Man upon the Rock of Albion Awakes,
'He listens to the sounds of War astonish'd & ashamed,
'He sees his Children mock at Faith and deny Providence.
'Therefore you must bind the Sheaves not by Nations or
    Families,
'You shall bind them in Three Classes, according to their
    Classes
'So shall you bind them, Separating What has been Mixed
'Since Men began to be Wove into Nations by Rahab &
    Tirzah,
'Since Albion's Death & Satan's Cutting off from our awful
    Fields,
'When under pretence to benevolence the Elect Subdu'd
    All
'From the Foundation of the World. The Elect is one Class:
    You

'Shall bind them separate: they cannot Believe in Eternal
    Life
'Except by Miracle & a New Birth. The other two Classes,
'The Reprobate who never cease to Believe, and the Re-
    deem'd
'Who live in doubts & fears perpetually tormented by the
    Elect,
'These you shall bind in a twin-bundle for the Consumma-
    tion:
'But the Elect must be saved from fires of Eternal Death,
'To be formed into the Churches of Beulah that they destroy
    not the Earth.
'For in every Nation & every Family the Three Classes are
    born,
'And in every Species of Earth, Metal, Tree, Fish, Bird &
    Beast.
'We form the Mundane Egg, that Spectres coming by fury
    or amity,
'All is the same, & every one remains in his own energy.
'Go forth Reapers with rejoicing; you sowed in tears,
'But the time of your refreshing cometh: only a little mo-
    ment
'Still abstain from pleasure & rest in the labours of eternity,
'And you shall Reap the whole Earth from Pole to Pole,
    from Sea to Sea,
'Beginning at Jerusalem's Inner Court, Lambeth, ruin'd
    and given
'To the detestable Gods of Priam, to Apollo, and at the
    Asylum
'Given to Hercules, who labour in Tirzah's Looms for
    bread,
'Who set Pleasure against Duty, who Create Olympic
    crowns
'To make Learning a burden & the Work of the Holy
    Spirit, Strife:

'The Thor & cruel Odin who first rear'd the Polar Caves.

'Lambeth mourns, calling Jerusalem: she weeps & looks
abroad

'For the Lord's coming, that Jerusalem may overspread all
Nations.

'Crave not for the mortal & perishing delights, but leave
them

'To the weak, and pity the weak as your infant care. Break
not

'Forth in your wrath, lest you also are vegetated by Tirzah.

'Wait till the Judgement is past, till the Creation is con-
sumed,

'And then rush forward with me into the glorious spiritual

'Vegetation, the Supper of the Lamb & his Bride, and the

'Awakening of Albion our friend and ancient companion.'

So Los spoke. But lightnings of discontent broke on all sides
round

And murmurs of thunder rolling heavy long & loud over the
mountains,

While Los call'd his Sons around him to the Harvest & the
Vintage.

Thou seest the Constellations in the deep & woundrous
Night:

They rise in order and continue their immortal courses

Upon the mountains & in vales with harp & heavenly song,

With flute & clarion, with cups & measures fill'd with foam-
ing wine.

Glitt'ring the streams reflect the Vision of beatitude,

And the calm Ocean joys beneath & smooths his awful
waves:

28

These are the Sons of Los, & these the Labourers of the
Vintage.

Thou seest the gorgeous clothed Flies that dance & sport in
      summer
Upon the sunny brooks & meadows: every one the dance
Knows in its intricate mazes of delight artful to weave:
Each one to sound his instruments of music in the dance,
To touch each other & recede, to cross & change & return:
These are the Children of Los; thou seest the Trees on
      mountains,
The wind blows heavy, loud they thunder thro' the darksom
      sky,
Uttering prophecies & speaking instructive words to the sons
Of men: These are the Sons of Los: These the Visions of
      Eternity,
But we see only as it were the hem of their garments
When with our vegetable eyes we view these wondrous
      Visions.

There are Two Gates thro' which all Souls descend, One
      Southward
From Dover Cliff to Lizard Point, the other toward the
      North,
Caithness & rocky Durness, Pentland & John Groat's
      House.

The Souls descending to the Body wail on the right hand
Of Los, & those deliver'd from the Body on the left hand.
For Los against the east his force continually bends
Along the Valleys of Middlesex from Hounslow to Black-
      heath,
Lest those Three Heavens of Beulah should the Creation
      destroy;
And lest they should descend before the north & south
      Gates,
Groaning with pity, he among the wailing Scots laments.

And these the Labours of the Sons of Los in Allamanda

And in the City of Golgonooza & in Luban & around
The Lake of Udan-Adan in the Forests of Entuthon Beny-
  thon,
Where Souls incessant wail, being piteous Passions & De-
  sires
With neither lineament nor form, but like to wat'ry clouds
The Passions & Desires descend upon the hungry winds,
For such alone Sleepers remain, meer passion & appetite.
The Sons of Los clothe them & feed & provide houses &
  fields.

And every Generated Body in its inward form
Is a garden of delight & a building of magnificence,
Built by the Sons of Los in Bowlahoola & Allamanda:
And the herbs & flowers & furniture & beds & chambers
Continually woven in the Looms of Enitharmon's Daugh-
  ters,
In bright Cathedron's golden Dome with care & love &
  tears.
For the various Classes of Men are all mark'd out deter-
  minate
In Bowlahoola, & as the Spectres choose their affinities,
So they are born on Earth, & every Class is determinate:
But not by Natural, but by Spiritual power alone, Because
The Natural power continually seeks & tends to Destruc-
  tion,
Ending in Death, which would of itself be Eternal Death.
And all are Class'd by Spiritual & not by Natural power.

And every Natural Effect has a Spiritual Cause, and Not
A Natural; for a Natural Cause only seems: it is a Delusion
Or Ulro & a ratio of the perishing Vegetable Memory.

29

But the Wine-press of Los is eastward of Golgonooza before
  the Seat

Of Satan: Luvah laid the foundation & Urizen finish'd it in
    howling woe.

How red the sons & daughters of Luvah! here they tread
    the grapes:

Laughing & shouting, drunk with odours many fall o'er-
    wearied,

Drown'd in the wine is many a youth & maiden: those
    around

Lay them on skins of Tygers & of the spotted Leopard & the
    Wild Ass

Till they revive, or bury them in cool grots, making lamen-
    tation.

This Wine-press is call'd War on Earth: it is the Printing-
    Press

Of Los, and here he lays his words in order above the mor-
    tal brain,

As cogs are form'd in a wheel to turn the cogs of the adverse
    wheel.

Timbrels & violins sport round the Wine-presses; the little
    Seed,

The sportive Root, the Earth-worm, the gold Beetle, the
    wise Emmet

Dance round the Wine-presses of Luvah: the Centipede is
    there,

The ground Spider with many eyes, the Mole clothed in
    velvet,

The ambitious Spider in his sullen web, the lucky golden
    Spinner,

The Earwig arm'd, the tender Maggot, emblem of immor-
    tality,

The Flea, Louse, Bug, the Tape-Worm, all the Armies of
    Disease,

Visible or invisible to the slothful vegetating Man.

The slow Slug, the Grasshopper that sings & laughs and
    drinks:
Winter comes, he folds his slender bones without a murmur.
The cruel Scorpion is there, the Gnat, Wasp, Hornet & the
    Honey Bee,
The Toad & venomous Newt, the Serpent cloth'd in gems
    & gold.
They throw off their gorgeous raiment: they rejoice with
    loud jubilee
Around the Wine-presses of Luvah, naked & drunk with
    wine.

There is the Nettle that stings with soft down, and there
The indignant Thistle whose bitterness is bred in his milk,
Who feeds on contempt of his neighbour: there all the idle
    Weeds
That creep around the obscure places shew their various
    limbs
Naked in all their beauty dancing round the Wine-presses.

But in the Wine-presses the Human grapes sing not nor
    dance:
They howl & writhe in shoals of torment, in fierce flames
    consuming
In chains of iron & in dungeons circled with ceaseless fires,
In pits & dens & shades of death, in shapes of torment &
    woe:
The plates & screws & wracks & saws & cords & fires &
    cisterns,
The cruel joys of Luvah's Daughters, lacerating with knives
And whips their Victims, & the deadly sport of Luvah's
    Sons.

They dance around the dying & they drink the howl &
    groan,

They catch the shrieks in cups of gold, they hand them to
    one another:
These are the sports of love, & these the sweet delights of
    amorous play,
Tears of the grape, the death sweat of the cluster, the last
    sigh
Of the mild youth who listens to the lureing songs of Luvah.

But Allamanda, call'd on Earth Commerce, is the Culti-
    vated land
Around the City of Golgonooza in the Forests of Entuthon:
Here the Sons of Los labour against Death Eternal, through
    all
The Twenty-seven Heavens of Beulah in Ulro, Seat of
    Satan,
Which is the False Tongue beneath Beulah: it is the Sense
    of Touch.
The Plow goes forth in tempests & lightnings, & the Har-
    row cruel
In blights of the east, the heavy Roller follows in howlings
    of woe.

Urizen's sons here labour also, & here are seen the Mills
Of Theotormon on the verge of the Lake of Udan-Adan.
These are the starry voids of night & the depths & caverns
    of earth.
These Mills are oceans, clouds & waters ungovernable in
    their fury:
Here are the stars created & the seeds of all things planted,
And here the Sun & Moon recieve their fixed destinations.

But in Eternity the Four Arts, Poetry, Painting, Music
And Architecture, which is Science, are the Four Faces of
    Man.
Not so in Time & Space: there Three are shut out, and only
Science remains thro' Mercy, & by means of Science the
    Three

Become apparent in Time & Space in the Three Profes-
    sions,
Poetry in Religion: Music, Law: Painting, in Physic & Sur-
    gery:
That Man may live upon Earth till the time of his awaking.
And from these Three Sciences derives every Occupation of
    Men,
And Science is divided into Bowlahoola & Allamanda.

30

Some Sons of Los surround the Passions with porches of iron
    & silver,
Creating form & beauty around the dark regions of sorrow,
Giving to airy nothing a name and a habitation
Delightful, with bounds to the Infinite putting off the In-
    definite
Into most holy forms of Thought; such is the power of in-
    spiration.
They labour incessant with many tears & afflictions,
Creating the beautiful House for the piteous sufferer.

Others Cabinets richly fabricate of gold & ivory
For Doubts & fears unform'd & wretched & melancholy.
The little weeping Spectre stands on the threshold of Death
Eternal, and sometimes two Spectres like lamps quivering,
And often malignant they combat; heart-breaking sorrowful
    & piteous,
Antamon takes them into his beautiful flexible hands:
As the Sower takes the seed or as the Artist his clay
Or fine wax, to mould artful a model for golden ornaments.
The soft hands of Antamon draw the indelible line,
Form immortal with golden pen, such as the Spectre ad-
    miring

Puts on the sweet form; then smiles Antamon bright thro'
 his windows.
The Daughters of beauty look up from their Loom & pre-
 pare
The integument soft for its clothing with joy & delight.

But Theotormon & Sotha stand in the Gate of Luban
 anxious.
Their numbers are seven million & seven thousand & seven
 hundred.
They contend with the weak Spectres, they fabricate sooth-
 ing forms.
The Spectre refuses, he seeks cruelty: they create the crested
 Cock.
Terrified the Spectre screams & rushes in fear into their Net
Of kindness & compassion, & is born a weeping terror.
Or they create the Lion & Tyger in compassionate thunder-
 ings:
Howling the Spectres flee: they take refuge in Human linea-
 ments.

The Sons of Ozoth within the Optic Nerve stand fiery glow-
 ing,
And the number of his Sons is eight millions & eight.
They give delights to the man unknown; artificial riches
They give to scorn, & their possessors to trouble & sorrow &
 care,
Shutting the sun & moon & stars & trees & clouds & waters
And hills out from the Optic Nerve, & hardening it into a
 bone
Opake and like the black pebble on the enraged beach,
While the poor indigent is like the diamond which, tho'
 cloth'd
In rugged covering in the mine, is open all within
And in his hallow'd center holds the heavens of bright eter-
 nity.

Ozoth here builds walls of rocks against the surging sea,
And timbers crampt with iron cramps bar in the joys of life
From fell destruction in the Spectrous cunning or rage. He
    Creates
The speckled Newt, the Spider & Beetle, the Rat & Mouse,
The Badger & Fox: they worship before his feet in tremb-
    ling fear.

But others of the Sons of Los build Moments & Minutes &
    Hours
And Days & Months & Years & Ages & Periods, wondrous
    buildings;
And every Moment has a Couch of gold for soft repose,
(A Moment equals a pulsation of the artery),
And between every two Moments stands a Daughter of
    Beulah
To feed the Sleepers on their Couches with maternal care.
And every Minute has an azure Tent with silken Veils:
And every Hour has a bright golden Gate carved with skill:
And every Day & Night has Walls of brass & Gates of ada-
    mant,
Shining like precious Stones & ornamented with appro-
    priate signs:
And every Month a silver paved Terrace builded high:
And every Year invulnerable Barriers with high Towers:
And every Age is Moated deep with Bridges of silver & gold:
And every Seven Ages is Incircled with a Flaming Fire.
Now Seven Ages is mounting to Two Hundred Years.
Each has its Guard, each Moment, Minute, Hour, Day,
    Month & Year.
All are the work of Fairy hands of the Four Elements:
The Guard are Angels of Providence on duty evermore.
Every Time less than a pulsation of the artery
Is equal in its period & value to Six Thousand Years,

For in this Period the Poet's Work is Done, and all the Great
Events of Time start forth & are conciev'd in such a Period,
Within a Moment, a Pulsation of the Artery.

The sky is an immortal Tent built by the Sons of Los:
And every Space that a Man views around his dwelling-
   place
Standing on his own roof or in his garden on a mount
Of twenty-five cubits in height, such space is his Universe:
And on its verge the Sun rises & sets, the Clouds bow
To meet the flat Earth & the Sea in such an order'd Space:
The Starry heavens reach no further, but here bend and set
On all sides, & the two Poles turn on their valves of gold;
And if he move his dwelling-place, his heavens also move
Where'er he goes, & all his neighbourhood bewail his loss.
Such are the Spaces called Earth & such its dimension.
As to that false appearance which appears to the reasoner
As of a Globe rolling thro' Voidness, it is a delusion of Ulro.
The Microscope knows not of this nor the Telescope: they
   alter
The ratio of the Spectator's Organs, but leave Objects un-
   touch'd.
For every Space larger than a red Globule of Man's blood
Is visionary, and is created by the Hammer of Los:
And every Space smaller than a Globule of Man's blood
   opens
Into Eternity of which this vegetable Earth is but a shadow.
The red Globule is the unwearied Sun by Los created
To measure Time and Space to mortal Men every morning.
Bowlahoola & Allamanda are placed on each side
Of that Pulsation & that Globule, terrible their power.

But Rintrah & Palamabron govern over Day & Night
In Allamanda & Entuthon Benython where Souls wail,

Where Orc incessant howls, burning in fires of Eternal
      Youth,
Within the vegetated mortal Nerves; for every Man born is
      joined
Within into One mighty Polypus, and this Polypus is Orc.

But in the Optic vegetative Nerves, Sleep was transformed
To Death in old time by Satan the father of Sin & Death:
And Satan is the Spectre of Orc, & Orc is the generate
      Luvah.

But in the Nerves of the Nostrils, Accident being formed
Into Substance & Principle by the cruelties of Demonstra-
      tion
It became Opake & Indefinite, but the Divine Saviour
Formed it into a Solid by Los's Mathematic power.
He named the Opake, Satan: he named the Solid, Adam.

And in the Nerves of the Ear (for the Nerves of the Tongue
      are closed)
On Albion's Rock Los stands creating the glorious Sun each
      morning,
And when unwearied in the evening, he creates the Moon,
Death to delude, who all in terror at their splendor leaves
His prey, while Los appoints & Rintrah & Palamabron
      guide
The Souls clear from the Rock of Death, that Death himself
      may wake
In his appointed season when the ends of heaven meet.

Then Los conducts the Spirits to be Vegetated into
Great Golgonooza, free from the four iron pillars of Satan's
      Throne,
(Temperance, Prudence, Justice, Fortitude, the four pillars
      of tyranny)
That Satan's Watch-Fiends touch them not before they
      Vegetate.

But Enitharmon and her Daughters take the pleasant charge
To give them to their lovely heavens till the Great Judgment
    Day:
Such is their lovely charge. But Rahab & Tirzah pervert
Their mild influences; therefore the Seven Eyes of God walk
    round
The Three Heavens of Ulro where Tirzah & her Sisters
Weave the black Woof of Death upon Entuthon Benython,
In the Vale of Surrey where Horeb terminates in Rephaim.
The stamping feet of Zelophehad's Daughters are cover'd
    with Human gore
Upon the treddles of the Loom: they sing to the winged
    shuttle.
The River rises above his banks to wash the Woof:
He takes it in his arms; he passes it in strength thro' his
    current;
The veil of human miseries is woven over the Ocean
From the Atlantic to the Great South Sea, the Erythrean.

Such is the World of Los, the labour of six thousand years.
Thus Nature is a Vision of the Science of the Elohim.

END OF THE FIRST BOOK

JERUSALEM

The Emanation of the Giant Albion

Written and etched 1804–1820

From *Chapter Four*

Los first broke silence & began to utter his love:

'O lovely Enitharmon! I behold thy graceful forms
'Moving beside me till, intoxicated with the woven laby-
    rinth
'Of beauty & perfection, my wild fibres shoot in veins
'Of blood thro' all my nervous limbs; soon overgrown in
    roots
'I shall be closed from thy sight; sieze therefore in thy hand
'The small fibres as they shoot around me, draw out in pity
'And let them run on the winds of thy bosom: I will fix them
'With pulsations; we will divide them into Sons & Daugh-
    ters
'To live in thy Bosom's translucence as in an eternal morn-
    ing.'

Enitharmon answer'd: 'No! I will sieze thy Fibres & weave
'Them, not as thou wilt, but as I will; for I will Create
'A round Womb beneath my bosom, lest I also be over-
    woven
'With Love; be thou assured I never will be thy slave.
'Let Man's delight be Love, but Woman's delight be Pride.
'In Eden our Loves were the same; here they are opposite.
'I have Loves of my own; I will weave them in Albion's
    Spectre.
'Cast thou in Jerusalem's shadows thy Loves, silk of liquid
'Rubies, Jacinths. Crysolites, issuing from thy Furnaces.
    While

'Jerusalem divides thy care, while thou carest for Jerusalem,
'Know that I never will be thine; also thou hidest Vala:
'From her these fibres shoot to shut me in a Grave.
'You are Albion's Victim; he has set his Daughter in your
    path.'

88

Los answer'd, sighing like the Bellows of his Furnaces:

'I care not! the swing of my Hammer shall measure the
    starry round.
'When in Eternity Man converses with Man, they enter
'Into each other's Bosom (which are Universes of delight)
'In mutual interchange, and first their Emanations meet
'Surrounded by their Children; if they embrace & comingle,
'The Human Four-fold Forms mingle also in thunders of
    Intellect;
'But if the Emanations mingle not, with storms & agitations
'Of earthquakes & consuming fires they roll apart in fear;
'For Man cannot unite with Man but by their Emanations
'Which stand both Male & Female at the Gates of each
    Humanity.
'How then can I ever again be united as Man with Man
'While thou, my Emanation, refusest my Fibres of domin-
    ion?
'When Souls mingle & join thro' all the Fibres of Brother-
    hood
'Can there be any secret joy on Earth greater than this?'

Enitharmon answer'd: 'This is Woman's World, nor need
    she any
'Spectre to defend her from Man. I will Create secret places,
'And the masculine names of the places, Merlin & Arthur.
'A triple Female Tabernacle for Moral Law I weave,
'That he who loves Jesus may loathe, terrified, Female love,

'Till God himself become a Male subservient to the Fe-
    male.'

She spoke in scorn & jealousy, alternate torments; and
So speaking she sat down on Sussex shore, singing lulling
Cadences & playing in sweet intoxication among the glist-
    ening
Fibres of Los, sending them over the Ocean eastward into
The realms of dark death. O perverse to thyself, contrar-
    ious
To thy own purposes! for when she began to weave,
Shooting out in sweet pleasure, her bosom in milky Love
Flow'd into the aching fibres of Los, yet contending against
    him,
In pride sending his Fibres over to her objects of jealousy
In the little lovely Allegoric Night of Albion's Daughters
Which stretch'd abroad, expanding east & west & north &
    south,
Thro' all the World of Erin & of Los & all their Children.

A sullen smile broke from the Spectre in mockery & scorn;
Knowing himself the author of their divisions & shrinkings,
    gratified
At their contentions, he wiped his tears, he wash'd his visage.

'The Man who respects Woman shall be despised by Wo-
    man,
'And deadly cunning & mean abjectness only shall enjoy
    them.
'For I will make their places of joy & love excrementitious,
'Continually building, continually destroying in Family
    feuds,
'While you are under the dominion of a jealous Female,
'Unpermanent for ever because of love & jealousy,
'You shall want all the Minute Particulars of Life.'

Thus joy'd the Spectre in the dusky fires of Los's Forge,
    eyeing
Enitharmon who at her shining Looms sings lulling caden-
    ces
While Los stood at his Anvil in wrath, the victim of their
    love
And hate, dividing the Space of Love with brazen Com-
    passes
In Golgonooza & in Udan-Adan & in Entuthon of Urizen.

The blow of his Hammer is Justice, the swing of his Ham-
    mer Mercy,
The force of Los's Hammer is eternal Forgiveness; but
His rage or his mildness were vain, she scatter'd his love on
    the wind
Eastward into her own Center, creating the Female Womb
In mild Jerusalem around the Lamb of God. Loud howl
The Furnaces of Los! loud roll the Wheels of Enith-
    armon!
The Four Zoas in all their faded majesty burst out in fury
And fire. Jerusalem took the Cup which foam'd in Vala's
    hand
Like the red Sun upon the mountains in the bloody day
Upon the Hermaphroditic Wine-presses of Love & Wrath.

89

Tho' divided by the Cross & Nails & Thorns & Spear
In cruelties of Rahab & Tirzan, permanent endure
A terrible indefinite Hermaphroditic form,
A Wine-press of Love & Wrath, double, Hermaphroditic,
Twelvefold in Allegoric pomp, in selfish holiness:
The Pharisaion, the Grammateis, the Presbiterion,
The Archiereus, the Iereus, the Saddusaion: double
Each withoutside of the other, covering eastern heaven.

Thus was the Covering Cherub reveal'd, majestic image
Of Selfhood, Body put off, the Antichrist accursed,
Cover'd with precious stones: a Human Dragon terrible
And bright stretch'd over Europe & Asia gorgeous.
In three nights he devour'd the rejected corse of death.

His Head, dark, deadly, in its Brain incloses a reflexion
Of Eden all perverted: Egypt on the Gihon, many tongued
And many mouth'd Ethiopia, Lybia, the Sea of Rephaim.
Minute Particulars in slavery I behold among the brick-
    kilns
Disorganiz'd; & there is Pharoh in his iron Court
And the Dragon of the River & the Furnaces of iron.
Outwoven from Thames & Tweed & Severn, awful streams,
Twelve ridges of Stone frown over all the Earth in tyrant
    pride,
Frown over each River, stupendous Works of Albion's
    Druid Sons,
And Albion's Forests of Oaks cover'd the Earth from Pole to
    Pole.

His Bosom wide reflects Moab & Ammon on the River
Pison, since call'd Arnon; there is Heshbon beautiful,
The Rocks of Rabbath on the Arnon & the Fish-pools of
    Heshbon
Whose currents flow into the Dead Sea by Sodom & Go-
    morra.
Above his Head high arching Wings, black, fill'd with Eyes,
Spring upon iron sinews from the Scapulae & Os Humeri:
There Israel in bondage to his Generalizing Gods,
Molech & Chemosh; & in his left breast is Philistea,
In Druid Temples over the whole Earth with Victim's Sa-
    crifice
From Gaza to Damascus, Tyre & Sidon, & the Gods
Of Javan thro' the Isles of Grecia & all Europe's Kings,

Where Hiddekel pursues his course among the rocks.
Two Wings spring from his ribs of brass, starry, black as
        night,
But translucent their blackness as the dazling of gems.

His Loins inclose Babylon on Euphrates beautiful
And Rome in sweet Hesperia: there Israel scatter'd abroad
In martyrdoms & slavery I behold, ah vision of sorrow!
Inclosed by eyeless Wings, glowing with fire as the iron
Heated in the Smith's forge, but cold the wind of their dread
        fury.

But in the midst of a devouring Stomach, Jerusalem
Hidden within the Covering Cherub, as in a Tabernacle
Of threefold workmanship, in allegoric delusion & woe:
There the Seven Kings of Canaan & Five Baalim of Philis-
        tea,
Sihon & Og, the Anakim & Emim, Nephilim & Gibbor-
        im,
From Babylon to Rome; & the Wings spread from Japan,
Where the Red Sea terminates the World of Generation &
        Death,
To Ireland's farthest rocks, where Giants builded their
        Causeway,
Into the Sea of Rephaim, but the Sea o'erwhelm'd them
        all.

A Double Female now appear'd within the Tabernacle,
Religion hid in War, a Dragon red & hidden Harlot
Each within other, but without, a Warlike Mighty-one
Of dreadful power sitting upon Horeb, pondering dire
And mighty preparations, mustering multitudes innumer-
        able
Of warlike sons among the sands of Midian & Aram.
For multitudes of those who sleep in Alla descend,
Lured by his warlike symphonies of tabret, pipe & harp,

Burst the bottoms of the Graves & Funeral Arks of Beulah.
Wandering in that unknown Night beyond the silent Grave
They become One with the Antichrist & are absorb'd in
    him.

90

The Feminine separates from the Masculine & both from
    Man,
Ceasing to be His Emanations, Life to Themselves assum-
    ing:
And while they circumscribe his Brain & while they circum-
    scribe
His Heart & while they circumscribe his Loins, a Veil &
    Net
Of Veins of red Blood grows around them like a scarlet robe
Covering them from the sight of Man, like the woven Veil of
    Sleep
Such as the Flowers of Beulah weave to be their Funeral
    Mantles;
But dark, opake, tender to touch, & painful & agonizing
To the embrace of love & to the mingling of soft fibres
Of tender affection, that no more the Masculine mingles
With the Feminine, but the Sublime is shut out from the
    Pathos
In howling torment, to build stone walls of separation, com-
    pelling
The Pathos to weave curtains of hiding secresy from the
    torment.

Bowen & Conwenna stood on Skiddaw cutting the Fibres
Of Benjamin from Chester's River; loud the River, loud the
    Mersey
And the Ribble thunder into the Irish sea as the Twelve
    Sons
Of Albion drank & imbibed the Life & eternal Form of
    Luvah;

Cheshire & Lancashire & Westmoreland groan in anguish
As they cut out the fibres from the Rivers; he sears them
with hot
Iron of his Forge & fixes them into Bones of chalk & Rock.
Conwenna sat above; with solemn cadences she drew
Fibres of life out from the Bones into her golden Loom.
Hand had his Furnace on Highgate's heights & it reach'd
To Brockley Hills across the Thames; he with double Boadi-
cea
In cruel pride cut Reuben apart from the Hills of Surrey,
Comingling with Luvah & with the Sepulcher of Luvah.
For the Male is a Furnace of beryll, the Female is a golden
Loom.

Los cries: 'No Individual ought to appropriate to Himself
'Or to his Emanation any of the Universal Characteristics
'Of David or of Eve, of the Woman or of the Lord,
'Of Reuben or of Benjamin, of Joseph or Judah or Levi.
'Those who dare appropriate to themselves Universal Attri-
butes
'Are the Blasphemous Selfhoods, & must be broken asunder.
'A Vegetated Christ & a Virgin Eve are the Hermaphro-
ditic
'Blasphemy; by his Maternal Birth he is that Evil-One
'And his Maternal Humanity must be put off Eternally,
'Lest the Sexual Generation swallow up Regeneration.
'Come Lord Jesus, take on thee the Satanic Body of Holi-
ness!'

So Los cried in the Valleys of Middlesex in the Spirit of
Prophecy,
While in Selfhood Hand & Hyle & Bowen & Skofeld appro-
priate
The Divine Names, seeking to Vegetate the Divine Vision
In a corporeal and ever dying Vegetation & Corruption;

Mingling with Luvah in One, they become One Great
    Satan.

Loud scream the Daughters of Albion beneath the Tongs &
    Hammer,
Dolorous are their lamentations in the burning Forge.
They drink Reuben & Benjamin as the iron drinks the fire:
They are red hot with cruelty, raving along the Banks of
    Thames
And on Tyburn's Brook among the howling Victims in
    loveliness,
While Hand & Hyle condense the Little-ones & erect them
    into
A mighty Temple even to the stars; but they Vegetate
Beneath Los's Hammer, that Life may not be blotted out.

For Los said: 'When the Individual appropriates Univer-
    sality
'He divides into Male & Female, & when the Male & Fe-
    male
'Appropriate Individuality they become an Eternal Death.
'Hermaphroditic worshippers of a God of cruelty & law,
'Your Slaves & Captives you compell to worship a God of
    Mercy!
'These are the Demonstrations of Los & the blows of my
    mighty Hammer.'

So Los spoke. And the Giants of Albion, terrified &
    ashamed
With Los's thunderous Words began to build trembling
    rocking Stones,
For his Words roll in thunders & lightnings among the Tem-
    ples
Terrified rocking to and fro upon the earth, & sometimes
Resting in a Circle in Malden or in Strathness or Dura,
Plotting to devour Albion & Los the friend of Albion,

Denying in private, mocking God & Eternal Life, & in Pub-
lic

Collusion calling themselves Deists, Worshipping the Mater-
nal

Humanity, calling it Nature and Natural Religion.

But still the thunder of Los peals loud, & thus the thunders
cry:

'These beautiful Witchcrafts of Albion are gratifyd by
Cruelty.

91

'It is easier to forgive an Enemy than to forgive a Friend.

'The man who permits you to injure him deserves your
vengeance:

'He also will recieve it; go Spectre! obey my most secret
desire

'Which thou knowest without my speaking. Go to these
Fiends of Righteousness,

'Tell them to obey their Humanities & not pretend Holiness

'When they are murderers: as far as my Hammer & Anvil
permit.

'Go, tell them that the Worship of God is honouring his
gifts

'In other men & loving the greatest men best, each accord-
ing

'To his Genius which is the Holy Ghost in Man; there is no
other

'God than that God who is the intellectual fountain of Hu-
manity.

'He who envies or calumniates, which is murder & cruelty,

'Murders the Holy-one. Go, tell them this, & overthrow
their cup,

'Their bread, their altar-table, their incense & their oath,

'Their marriage & their baptism, their burial & consecration.

'I have tried to make friends by corporeal gifts but have only
'Made enemies. I never made friends but by spiritual gifts,
'By severe contentions of friendship & the burning fire of
    thought.

'He who would see the Divinity must see him in his Children,
'One first, in friendship & love, then a Divine Family, & in
    the midst

'Jesus will appear; so he who wishes to see a Vision, a perfect Whole,
'Must see it in its Minute Particulars, Organized, & not as
    thou,

'O Fiend of Righteousness, pretendest; thine is a Disorganized
'And snowy cloud, brooder of tempests & destructive War.

'You smile with pomp & rigor, you talk of benevolence &
    virtue;

'I act with benevolence & Virtue & get murder'd time after
    time.

'You accumulate Particulars & murder by analyzing, that
    you

'May take the aggregate, & you call the aggregate Moral
    Law,

'And you call that swell'd & bloated Form a Minute Particular;

'But General Forms have their vitality in Particulars, &
    every

'Particular is a Man, a Divine Member of the Divine
    Jesus.'

So Los cried at his Anvil in the horrible darkness weeping.

The Spectre builded stupendous Works, taking the Starry
    Heavens

Like to a curtain & folding them according to his will,
Repeating the Smaragdine Table of Hermes to draw Los
    down
Into the Indefinite, refusing to believe without demonstra-
    tion.
Los reads the Stars of Albion, the Spectre reads the Voids
Between the Stars among the arches of Albion's Tomb
    sublime,
Rolling the Sea in rocky paths, forming Leviathan
And Behemoth, the War by Sea, enormous & the War
By Land astounding, erecting pillars in the deepest Hell
To reach the heavenly arches. Los beheld undaunted,
    furious,
His heav'd Hammer; he swung it round & at one blow
In unpitying ruin driving down the pyramids of pride,
Smiting the Spectre on his Anvil & the integuments of his
    Eye
And Ear unbinding in dire pain, with many blows
Of strict severity self-subduing, & with many tears labour-
    ing.

Then he sent forth the Spectre: all his pyramids were grains
Of sand, & his pillars dust on the fly's wing, & his starry
Heavens a moth of gold & silver, mocking his anxious grasp.
Thus Los alter'd his Spectre, & every Ratio of his Reason
He alter'd time after time with dire pain & many tears
Till he had completely divided him into a separate space.

Terrified Los sat to behold, trembling & weeping & howl-
    ing:
'I care not whether a Man is Good or Evil; all that I care
'Is whether he is a Wise Man or a Fool. Go, put off Holi-
    ness
'And put on Intellect, or my thund'rous Hammer shall
    drive thee

'To wrath which thou condemnest, till thou obey my voice.'

So Los terrified cries, trembling & weeping & howling:
        'Beholding,

92

'What do I see! The Briton, Saxon, Roman, Norman amal-
        gamating
'In my Furnaces into One Nation, the English, & taking
        refuge
'In the Loins of Albion. The Canaanite united with the
        fugitive
'Hebrew, whom she divided into Twelve & sold into Egypt,
'Then scatter'd the Egyptian & Hebrew to the four Winds.
'This sinful Nation Created in our Furnaces & Looms is
        Albion.'

So Los spoke. Enitharmon answer'd in great terror in Lam-
        beth's Vale:

'The Poet's Song draws to its period, & Enitharmon is no
        more;
'For if he be that Albion, I can never weave him in my
        Looms,
'But when he touches the first fibrous thread, like filmy dew
'My Looms will be no more & I annihilate vanish for ever.
'Then thou wilt Create another Female according to thy
        Will.'

Los answer'd swift as the shuttle of gold: 'Sexes must vanish
        & cease
'To be when Albion arises from his dread repose, O lovely
        Enitharmon:
'When all their Crimes, their Punishments, their Accusa-
        tions of Sin,

'All their Jealousies, Revenges, Murders, hidings of Cruelty
  in Deceit
'Appear only in the Outward Spheres of Visionary Space
  and Time,
'In the shadows of Possibility, by Mutual Forgiveness for
  evermore,
'And in the Vision & in the Prophecy, that we may Fore-
  see & Avoid
'The terrors of Creation & Redemption & Judgment: Be-
  holding them
'Display'd in the Emanative Visions of Canaan, in Jerusa-
  lem & in Shiloh
'And in the Shadows of Remembrance & in the Chaos of
  the Spectre,
'Amalek, Edom, Egypt, Moab, Ammon, Ashur, Philistea,
  around Jerusalem,
'Where the Druids rear'd their Rocky Circles to make per-
  manent Remembrance
'Of Sin, & the Tree of Good & Evil sprang from the Rocky
  Circle & Snake
'Of the Druid, along the Valley of Rephaim from Camber-
  well to Golgotha,
'And framed the Mundane Shell Cavernous in Length
  Breadth & Highth.'

93

Enitharmon heard. She rais'd her head like the mild Moon:

'O Rintrah! O Palamabron! What are your dire & awful
  purposes?
'Enitharmon's name is nothing before you; you forget all
  my Love.

'The Mother's love of obedience is forgotten, & you seek a
    Love
'Of the pride of dominion that will Divorce Ocalythron &
    Elynittria
'Upon East Moor in Derbyshire & along the Valleys of
    Cheviot.
'Could you Love me, Rintrah, if you Pride not in my Love?
'As Reuben found Mandrakes in the field & gave them to
    his Mother,
'Pride meets with Pride upon the Mountains in the stormy
    day,
'In that terrible Day of Rintrah's Plow & of Satan's driving
    the Team.
'Ah! then I heard my little ones weeping along the Valley.
'Ah! then I saw my beloved ones fleeing from my Tent.
'Merlin was like thee, Rintrah, among the Giants of Al-
    bion,
'Judah was like Palamabron. O Simeon! O Levi! ye fled
    away!
'How can I hear my little ones weeping along the Valley,
'Or how upon the distant Hills see my beloveds' Tents?'

Then Los again took up his speech as Enitharmon ceast:

'Fear not, my Sons, this Waking Death; he is become One
    with me.
'Behold him here! We shall not Die! we shall be united in
    Jesus.
'Will you suffer this Satan, this Body of Doubt that Seems
    but Is Not,
'To occupy the very threshold of Eternal Life? if Bacon,
    Newton, Locke
'Deny a Conscience in Man & the Communion of Saints &
    Angels,
'Contemning the Divine Vision & Fruition, Worshipping
    the Deus

'Of the Heathen, The God of This World, & the Goddess
    Nature,
'Mystery, Babylon the Great, The Druid Dragon & hidden
    Harlot,
'Is it not that Signal of the Morning which was told us in the
    Beginning?'

Thus they converse upon Mam-Tor, the Graves thunder
    under their feet.

94

Albion cold lays on his Rock: storms & snows beat round
    him,
Beneath the Furnaces & the starry Wheels & the Immortal
    Tomb:
Howling winds cover him: roaring seas dash furious against
    him:
In the deep darkness broad lightnings glare, long thunders
    roll.

The weeds of Death inwrap his hands & feet, blown inces-
    sant
And wash'd incessant by the for-ever restless sea-waves
    foaming abroad
Upon the white Rock. England, a Female Shadow, as dead-
    ly damps
Of the Mines of Cornwall & Derbyshire, lays upon his
    bosom heavy,
Moved by the wind in volumes of thick cloud, returning,
    folding round
His loins & bosom, unremovable by swelling storms & loud
    rending
Of enraged thunders. Around them the Starry Wheels of
    their Giant Sons

Revolve, & over them the Furnaces of Los, & the Immortal
    Tomb around,
Erin sitting in the Tomb to watch them unceasing night and
    day:
And the Body of Albion was closed apart from all Nations.

Over them the famish'd Eagle screams on boney Wings, and
    around
Them howls the Wolf of famine; deep heaves the Ocean
    black, thundering
Around the wormy Garments of Albion, then pausing in
    deathlike silence.

Time was Finished! The Breath Divine Breathed over Al-
    bion
Beneath the Furnaces & starry Wheels and in the Immortal
    Tomb,
And England, who is Brittannia, awoke from Death on Al-
    bion's bosom:
She awoke pale & cold; she fainted seven times on the Body
    of Albion.

'O pitious Sleep, O pitious Dream! O God, O God awake!
    I have slain
'In Dreams of Chastity & Moral Law: I have Murdered
    Albion! Ah!
'In Stone-henge & on London Stone & in the Oak Groves
    of Malden
'I have Slain him in my Sleep with the Knife of the Druid.
    O England!
'O all ye Nations of the Earth, behold ye the Jealous Wife!
'The Eagle & the Wolf & Monkey & Owl & the King &
    Priest were there.'

95

Her voice pierc'd Albion's clay cold ear; he moved upon the
    Rock.

The Breath Divine went forth upon the morning hills. Albion mov'd

Upon the Rock, he open'd his eyelids in pain, in pain he mov'd

His stony members, he saw England. Ah! shall the Dead live again?

The Breath Divine went forth over the morning hills. Albion rose

In anger, the wrath of God breaking, bright flaming on all sides around

His awful limbs; into the Heavens he walked, clothed in flames,

Loud thund'ring, with broad flashes of flaming lightning & pillars

Of fire, speaking the Words of Eternity in Human Forms, in direful

Revolutions of Action & Passion, thro' the Four Elements on all sides

Surrounding his awful Members. Thou seest the Sun in heavy clouds

Struggling to rise above the Mountains; in his burning hand

He takes his Bow, then chooses out his arrows of flaming gold;

Murmuring the Bowstring breathes with ardor! clouds roll round the

Horns of the wide Bow, loud sounding winds sport on the mountain brows,

Compelling Urizen to his Furrow & Tharmas to his Sheepfold

And Luvah to his Loom: Urthona he beheld, mighty labouring at

His Anvil, in the Great Spectre Los unwearied labouring & weeping:

Therefore the Sons of Eden praise Urthona's Spectre in songs,

Because he kept the Divine Vision in time of trouble.

2ing,

As the Sun & Moon lead forward the Visions of Heaven &
    Earth,
England, who is Brittannia, enter'd Albion's bosom rejoic-
    ing,
Rejoicing in his indignation, adoring his wrathful rebuke.
She who adores not your frowns will only loathe your smiles.

96

As the Sun & Moon lead forward the Visions of Heaven &
    Earth,
England, who is Brittannia, entered Albion's bosom rejoic-
    ing.

Then Jesus appeared standing by Albion as the Good
    Shepherd
By the lost Sheep that he hath found, & Albion knew that it
Was the Lord, the Universal Humanity; & Albion saw his
    Form
A Man, & they conversed as Man with Man in Ages of
    Eternity.
And the Divine Appearance was the likeness & similitude of
    Los.

Albion said: 'O Lord, what can I do? my Selfhood cruel
'Marches against thee, deceitful, from Sinai & from Edom
'Into the Wilderness of Judah, to meet thee in his pride.
'I behold the Visions of my deadly Sleep of Six Thousand
    Years
'Dazling around thy skirts like a Serpent of precious stones
    & gold.
'I know it is my Self, O my Divine Creator & Redeemer.'
Jesus replied: 'Fear not Albion: unless I die thou canst not
    live;
'But if I die I shall arise again & thou with me.
'This is Friendship & Brotherhood: without it Man Is Not.

So Jesus spoke: the Covering Cherub coming on in darkness
Overshadow'd them, & Jesus said: 'Thus do Men in Eternity
'One for another to put off, by forgiveness, every sin.'

Albion reply'd: 'Cannot Man exist without Mysterious
'Offering of Self for Another? is this Friendship & Brotherhood?
'I see thee in the likeness & similitude of Los my Friend.'

Jesus said: 'Wouldest thou love one who never died
'For thee, or ever die for one who had not died for thee?
'And if God dieth not for Man & giveth not himself
'Eternally for Man, Man could not exist; for Man is Love
'As God is Love: every kindness to another is a little Death
'In the Divine Image, nor can Man exist but by Brotherhood.'

So saying the Cloud overshadowing divided them asunder.
Albion stood in terror, not for himself but for his Friend
Divine; & Self was lost in the contemplation of faith
And wonder at the Divine Mercy & at Los's sublime honour.

'Do I sleep amidst danger to Friends? O my Cities & Counties,
'Do you sleep? rouze up, rouze up! Eternal Death is abroad!'

So Albion spoke & threw himself into the Furnaces of affliction.
All was a Vision, all a Dream: the Furnaces became
Fountains of Living Waters flowing from the Humanity Divine.
And all the Cities of Albion rose from their Slumbers, and All

The Sons & Daughters of Albion on soft clouds, waking
    from Sleep.
Soon all around remote the Heavens burnt with flaming
    fires,
And Urizen & Luvah & Tharmas & Urthona arose into
Albion's Bosom. Then Albion stood before Jesus in the
    Clouds
Of Heaven, Fourfold among the Visions of God in Eternity.

97

'Awake, Awake, Jerusalem! O lovely Emanation of Albion,
'Awake and overspread all nations as in Ancient Time;
'For lo! the Night of Death is past and the Eternal Day
'Appears upon our Hills. Awake, Jerusalem, and come
    away!'

So spake the Vision of Albion, & in him so spake in my
    hearing
The Universal Father. Then Albion stretch'd his hand into
    Infinitude
And took his Bow. Fourfold the Vision; for bright beaming
    Urizen
Lay'd his hand on the South & took a breathing Bow of
    carved Gold:
Luvah his hand stretch'd to the East & bore a Silver Bow,
    bright shining:
Tharmas Westward a Bow of Brass, pure flaming, richly
    wrought:
Urthona Northward in thick storms a Bow of Iron, terrible
    thundering.

And the Bow is a Male & Female, & the Quiver of the
    Arrows of Love
Are the Children of this Bow, a Bow of Mercy & Loving
    kindness laying

Open the hidden Heart in Wars of mutual Benevolence,
    Wars of Love:
And the Hand of Man grasps firm between the Male &
    Female Loves.
And he Clothed himself in Bows & Arrows, in awful state,
    Fourfold,
In the midst of his Twenty-eight Cities, each with his Bow
    breathing.

98

Then each an Arrow flaming from his Quiver fitted care-
    fully:
They drew fourfold the unreprovable String, bending thro'
    the wide Heavens
The horned Bow Fourfold; loud sounding flew the flaming
    Arrow fourfold.

Murmuring the Bowstring breathes with ardor. Clouds roll
    round the horns
Of the wide Bow; loud sounding Winds sport on the Moun-
    tains' Brows.
The Druid Spectre was Annihilate, loud thund'ring, rejoic-
    ing terrific, vanishing,
Fourfold Annihilation; & at the clangor of the Arrows of
    Intellect
The innumerable Chariots of the Almighty appear'd in
    Heaven,
And Bacon & Newton & Locke, & Milton & Shakspear &
    Chaucer,
A Sun of blood red wrath surrounding heaven, on all sides
    around,
Glorious, incomprehensible by Mortal Man & each Char-
    iot was Sexual Threefold.

And every Man stood Fourfold; each Four Faces had: One
    to the West,

One toward the East, One to the South, One to the North,
the Horses Fourfold.

And the dim Chaos brighten'd beneath, above, around:
Eyed as the Peacock,

According to the Human Nerves of Sensation, the Four
Rivers of the Water of Life.

South stood the Nerves of the Eye; East, in Rivers of bliss,
the Nerves of the

Expansive Nostrils; West flow'd the Parent Sense, the
Tongue; North stood

The labyrinthine Ear: Circumscribing & Circumcising the
excrementitious

Husk & Covering, into Vacuum evaporating, revealing the
lineaments of Man,

Driving outward the Body of Death in an Eternal Death &
Resurrection,

Awaking it to Life among the Flowers of Beulah, rejoicing
in Unity

In the Four Senses, in the Outline, the Circumference &
Form, for ever

In Forgiveness of Sins which is Self Annihilation; it is the
Covenant of Jehovah.

The Four Living Creatures, Chariots of Humanity Divine
Incomprehensible,

In beautiful Paradises expand. These are the Four Rivers of
Paradise

And the Four Faces of Humanity, fronting the Four Car-
dinal Points

Of Heaven, going forward, forward irresistible from Eter-
nity to Eternity.

And they conversed together in Visionary forms dramatic
which bright

Redounded from their Tongues in thunderous majesty, in
    Visions

In new Expanses, creating exemplars of Memory and of
    Intellect,

Creating Space, Creating Time, according to the wonders
    Divine

Of Human Imagination throughout all the Three Regions
    immense

Of Childhood, Manhood & Old Age; & the all tremendous
    unfathomable Non Ens

Of Death was seen in regenerations terrific or complacent,
    varying

According to the subject of discourse; & every Word &
    every Character

Was Human according to the Expansion or Contraction, the
    Translucence or

Opakeness of Nervous fibres: such was the variation of Time
    & Space

Which vary according as the Organs of Perception vary; &
    they walked

To & fro in Eternity as One Man, reflecting each in each &
    clearly seen

And seeing, according to fitness & order. And I heard Jeho-
    vah speak

Terrific from his Holy Place, & saw the Words of the Mutual
    Covenant Divine

Of Chariots of gold & jewels, with Living Creatures, starry
    & flaming

With every Colour, Lion, Tyger, Horse, Elephant, Eagle,
    Dove, Fly, Worm

And the all wondrous Serpent clothed in gems & rich array,
    Humanize

In the Forgiveness of Sins according to thy Covenant, Jeho-
    vah. They Cry:

'Where is the Covenant of Priam, the Moral Virtues of the
    Heathen?
'Where is the Tree of Good & Evil that rooted beneath the
    cruel heel
'Of Albion's Spectre, the Patriarch Druid? where are all his
    Human Sacrifice
'For Sin in War & in the Druid Temples of the Accuser of
    Sin, beneath
'The Oak Groves of Albion that cover'd the whole Earth
    beneath his Spectre?
'Where are the Kingdoms of the World & all their glory
    that grew on Desolation,
'The Fruit of Albion's Poverty Tree, when the Triple
    Headed Gog-Magog Giant
'Of Albion Taxed the Nations into Desolation & then gave
    the Spectrous Oath?'
Such is the Cry from all the Earth, from the living Creatures
    of the Earth
And from the great City of Golgonooza in the Shadowy
    Generation,
And from the Thirty-two Nations of the Earth among the
    Living Creatures.

99

All Human Forms identified, even Tree, Metal, Earth &
    Stone: all
Human Forms identified, living, going forth & returning
    wearied
Into the Planetary lives of Years, Months, Days & Hours;
    reposing,
And then Awaking into his Bosom in the Life of Immortality.

And I heard the Name of their Emanations: they are
    named Jerusalem.

THE END OF THE SONG OF JERUSALEM

From THE GATES OF PARADISE
1793–1818

Epilogue

To The Accuser who is
The God of This World

Truly, My Satan, thou art but a Dunce,
And dost not know the Garment from the Man.
Every Harlot was a Virgin once,
Nor can'st thou ever change Kate into Nan.

Tho' thou art Worship'd by the Names Divine
Of Jesus & Jehovah, thou art still
The Son of Morn in weary Night's decline,
The lost Traveller's Dream under the Hill.

ANNOTATIONS TO DR. THORNTON'S 'NEW TRANSLATION OF THE LORD'S PRAYER' LONDON MDCCCXXVII

Written 1827

I look upon this as a Most Malignant & Artful attack upon the Kingdom of Jesus By the Classical Learned, thro' the Instrumentality of Dr. Thornton. The Greek & Roman Classics is the Antichrist. I say Is & not Are as most expressive & correct too. (*on the title-page*)

(*Those of Blake's subsequent annotations that refer to the text are printed after the relevant passages which are given in smaller type. On page 3 is Blake's own version of the Lord's Prayer; on the fly-leaf at the end is his paraphrase of Dr. Thornton's version.*)

Page iii
Doctor Johnson on the Bible: 'The Bible is the most difficult 'book in the world to comprehend, nor can it be understood at 'all by the unlearned, except through the aid of critical and 'explanatory notes.'

Christ & his Apostles were Illiterate Men; Cai(a)phas, Pilate & Herod were Learned.

Lord Byron on the Ethics of Christ: 'What made Socrates the 'greatest of men? His moral truths – his ethics. What proved 'Jesus Christ to be the son of God, hardly less than his miracles 'did? His moral precepts.'

If Morality was Christianity, Socrates was The Savior.

The Beauty of the Bible is that the most Ignorant & Simple Minds Understand it Best – Was Johnson hired to Pretend to Religious Terrors while he was an Infidel, or how was it?

Page iv

The only thing for Newtonian & Baconian Philosophers to Consider is this: Whether Jesus did not suffer himself to be Mock'd by Caesar's Soldiers Willingly, & to Consider this to all Eternity will be Comment Enough.

Page 1

(*Following remarks on the necessity for a new translation of the Bible.*)

Such things as these depend on the Fashion of the Age
In a book where all may Read, & ⎫
In a book which all may Read, & ⎬ are Equally Right.
In a book that all may Read ⎭
That Man who &c is equally so – The Man that & the Man which.

Men from their childhood have been so accustomed to mouth the Lord's Prayer, that they continue this through life, and call it 'Saying their Prayers'. . . .

It is the learned that Mouth, & not the Vulgar.

THE LORD'S PRAYER
Translated from the Greek, by Dr. Thornton

Come let us worship, and bow down, and kneel, before the Lord, our Maker. Psalm xcv.

O Father of Mankind, Thou, who dwellest in the highest of the Heavens, Reverenc'd be Thy Name.

May Thy Reign be, every where, proclaim'd so that Thy Will may be done upon the Earth, as it is in the Mansions of Heaven:

Grant unto me, and the whole world, day by day, an abundant supply of spiritual and corporeal Food:

Forgive us our transgressions against Thee, as we extend our Kindness, and Forgiveness, to all:

O God! abandon us not, when surrounded, by trials;

But preserve us from the Dominion of Satan: For Thine only, is the Sovereignty, the power, and the glory, throughout Eternity!!! Amen.

Lawful Bread, Bought with Lawful Money, & a Lawful Heaven, seen thro' a Lawful Telescope, by means of Lawful Window Light! The Holy Ghost, & whatever cannot be Taxed, is Unlawful & Witchcraft.

Spirits are Lawful, but not Ghosts; especially Royal Gin is Lawful Spirit. No Smuggling real British Spirit & Truth!

Page 2

Give us the Bread that is our due & Right, by taking away Money, or a Price, or Tax upon what is Common to all in thy Kingdom.

Page 3

Jesus, our Father, who art in thy heaven call'd by thy Name the Holy Ghost, Thy Kingdom on Earth is Not, nor thy Will done, but Satan's, who is God of this World, the Accuser. Let his Judgment be Forgiveness that he may be cursed on his own throne.

Give us This Eternal Day our own right Bread by taking away Money or debtor Tax & Value or Price, as (*words illegible*) have all the Common (*several words illegible*) among us. Every thing has as much right to Eternal Life as God, who is the Servant of Man. His Judgment shall be Forgiveness that he may be consum'd on his own Throne.

Leave us not in Parsimony, Satan's Kingdom; liberate us from the Natural Man & (*words illegible*) Kingdom.

For thine is the Kingdom & the Power & the Glory & not Caesar's or Satan's. Amen.

Page 5

Dim at best are the conceptions we have of the Supreme Being, who, as it were, keeps the human race in suspense, neither discovering, nor hiding Himself; . . .

a Female God!

Page 6
What is the Will of God we are ordered to obey? ... Let us
consider whose Will it is. ... It is the Will of our Maker. ... It is
finally the Will of Him, who is uncontrollably powerful. ...

So you See That God is just such a Tyrant as Augustus
Caesar; & is not this Good & Learned & Wise & Classical?

Fly-leaf

This is Saying the Lord's Prayer Backwards, which they
say Raises the devil.

Doctor Thornton's Tory Translation, Translated out of
its disguise in the Classical & Scotch languages into the
vulgar English.

Our Father Augustus Caesar, who art in these thy Sub-
stantial Astronomical Telescopic Heavens, Holiness to thy
Name or Title, & reverence to thy Shadow. Thy Kingship
come upon Earth first & then in Heaven. Give us day by
day our Real Taxed Substantial Money bought Bread;
deliver from the Holy Ghost whatever cannot be Taxed; for
all is debts & Taxes between Caesar & us & one another;
lead us not to read the Bible, but let our Bible be Virgil &
Shakspeare; & deliver us from Poverty in Jesus, that Evil
One. For thine is the Kingship, (or) Allegoric Godship, &
the Power, or War, & the Glory, or Law, Ages after Ages in
thy descendants; for God is only an Allegory of Kings &
nothing Else. Amen.

I swear that Basileia, βασιλεια, is not Kingdom but
Kingship. I, Nature, Hermaphroditic Priest & King, Live
in Real Substantial Natural Born Man, & that Spirit is the
Ghost of Matter or Nature, & God is The Ghost of the
Priest & King, who Exist, whereas God exists not except
from their Effluvia.

Here is Signed Two Names which are too Holy to be
Written.

Thus we see that the Real God is the Goddess Nature, & that God Creates nothing but what can be Touch'd & Weighed & Taxed & Measured; all else is Heresy & Rebellion against Caesar, Virgil's Only God – see Eclogue 1; for all this we Thank Dr. Thornton.

LETTERS

To the Revd. Dr. Trusler

Hercules Buildgs, Lambeth,
Augst. 16, 1799.

Revd. Sir,

I find more & more that my Style of Designing is a Species by itself, & in this which I send you have been compell'd by my Genius or Angel to follow where he led; if I were to act otherwise it would not fulfill the purpose for which alone I live, which is, in conjunction with such men as my friend Cumberland, to renew the lost Art of the Greeks.

I attempted every morning for a fortnight together to follow your Dictate, but when I found my attempts were in vain, resolv'd to shew an independence which I know will please an Author better than slavishly following the track of another, however admirable that track may be. At any rate, my Excuse must be: I could not do otherwise; it was out of my power!

I know I begged of you to give me your Ideas, & promised to build on them; here I counted without my host. I now find my mistake.

The Design I have Sent Is:

A Father, taking leave of his Wife & Child, Is watch'd by Two Fiends incarnate, with intention that when his back is turned they will murder the mother & her infant. If this is not Malevolence with a vengeance, I have never seen it on Earth; & if you approve of this, I have no doubt of giving you Benevolence with Equal Vigor, as also Pride & Humility, but cannot previously describe in words what I mean to Design, for fear I should Evaporate the Spirit of my Invention. But I hope that none of my Designs will be destitute of Infinite Particulars which will present themselves to the Contemplator. And tho' I call them Mine, I know that they are not Mine, being of the same opinion with Milton when he says That the Muse visits his Slumbers & awakes & governs his Song when Morn purples the East, & being also in the predicament of that prophet who says: I cannot go beyond the command of the Lord, to speak good or bad.

If you approve of my Manner, & it is agreeable to you, I would rather Paint Pictures in oil of the same dimensions than make Drawings, & on the same terms; by this means you will have a number of Cabinet pictures, which I flatter myself will not be unworthy of a Scholar of Rembrandt & Teniers, whom I have Studied no less than Rafael & Michael angelo. Please to send me your orders respecting this, & In my next Effort I promise more Expedition.

I am, Revd. Sir,
Your very humble servt.
WILLM. BLAKE.

To the Revd. Dr. Trusler

13 Hercules Buildings,
Lambeth,
August 23, 1799.

Revd. Sir,

I really am sorry that you are fall'n out with the Spiritual World, Especially if I should have to answer for it. I feel very sorry that your Ideas & Mine on Moral Painting differ so much as to have made you angry with my method of Study. If I am wrong, I am wrong in good company. I had hoped your plan comprehended All Species of this Art, & Especially that you would not regret that Species which gives Existence to Every other, namely, Visions of Eternity.

You say that I want somebody to Elucidate my Ideas. But you ought to know that What is Grand is necessarily obscure to Weak men. That which can be made Explicit to the Idiot is not worth my care. The wisest of the Ancients consider'd what is not too Explicit as the fittest for Instruction, because it rouzes the faculties to act. I name Moses, Solomon, Esop, Homer, Plato.

But as you have favor'd me with your remarks on my Design, permit me in return to defend it against a mistaken one, which is, That I have supposed Malevolence without a Cause. Is not Merit in one a Cause of Envy in another, & Serenity & Happiness & Beauty a Cause of Malevolence? But Want of Money & the Distress of A Thief can never be alledged as the Cause of his Thieving, for many honest people endure greater hardships with Fortitude. We must therefore seek the Cause elsewhere than in want of Money, for that is the Miser's passion, not the Thief's.

I have therefore proved your Reasonings Ill proportion'd, which you can never prove my figures to be; they are those of Michael Angelo, Rafael & the Antique, & of the best living Models. I percieve that your Eye is perverted by Caricature Prints, which ought not to abound so much as they do. Fun I love, but too much Fun is of all things the most loathsom. Mirth is better than Fun, & Happiness is better than Mirth. I feel that a Man may be happy in This World. And I know that This World Is a World of Imagination & Vision. I see Every thing I paint In This World, but Every body does not see alike. To the Eyes of a Miser a Guinea is more beautiful than the Sun, & a bag worn with the use of Money has more beautiful proportions than a Vine filled with Grapes. The tree which moves some to tears of joy is in the Eyes of others only a Green thing that stands in the way. Some See Nature all Ridicule & Deformity, & by these I shall not regulate my proportions; & Some Scarce see Nature at all. But to the Eyes of the Man of

Imagination, Nature is Imagination itself. As a man is, So he Sees. As the Eye is formed, such are its Powers. You certainly Mistake, when you say that the Visions of Fancy are not to be found in This World. To Me This World is all One continued Vision of Fancy or Imagination, & I feel Flatter'd when I am told so. What is it sets Homer, Virgil & Milton in so high a rank of Art? Why is the Bible more Entertaining & Instructive than any other book? Is it not because they are addressed to the Imagination, which is Spiritual Sensation, & but mediately to the Understanding or Reason? Such is True Painting, and such was alone valued by the Greeks & the best modern Artists. Consider what Lord Bacon says: 'Sense sends over to Imagination 'before Reason have judged, & Reason sends over to 'Imagination before the Decree can be acted.' See Advancemt. of Learning, Part 2, P. 47 of first Edition.

But I am happy to find a Great Majority of Fellow Mortals who can Elucidate My Visions, & Particularly they have been Elucidated by Children, who have taken a greater delight in contemplating my Pictures than I even hoped. Neither Youth nor Childhood is Folly or Incapacity. Some Children are Fools & so are some Old Men. But There is a vast Majority on the side of Imagination or Spiritual Sensation.

To Engrave after another Painter is infinitely more laborious than to Engrave one's own Inventions. And of the size you require my price has been Thirty Guineas, & I cannot afford to do it for less. I had Twelve for the Head I sent you as a specimen; but after my own designs I could do at least Six times the quantity of labour in the same time, which will account for the difference of price as also that Chalk Engraving is at least six times as laborious as Aqua tinta. I have no objection to Engraving after another Artist. Engraving is the profession I was apprenticed to, & should never have attempted to live by anything else, If orders had not come in for my Designs & Paintings, which I have the pleasure to tell you are Increasing Every Day. Thus If I am a Painter it is not to be attributed to Seeking after. But I am contented whether I live by Painting or Engraving.

I am, Revd. Sir, your very obedient servant,

WILLIAM BLAKE.

To George Cumberland

Hercules Buildings,
Lambeth,
Augst. 26, 1799.

Dear Cumberland,

I ought long ago to have written to you to thank you for your kind recommendation to Dr. Trusler, which, tho' it has fail'd of success, is not the less to be remember'd by me with Gratitude.

I have made him a Drawing in my best manner; he has sent it back with a Letter full of Criticisms, in which he says It accords not with his Intentions, which are to Reject all Fancy from his Work. How far he Expects to please, I cannot tell. But as I cannot paint Dirty rags & old shoes where I ought to place Naked Beauty or simple ornament, I despair of Ever pleasing one Class of Men. Unfortunately our authors of books are among this Class; how soon we Shall have a change for the better I cannot Prophecy. Dr. Trusler says: '*Your Fancy*, from what I have seen of it, & I have seen variety at Mr. Cumberland's, seems to be in the other world, or the World of Spirits, which accords not with my Intentions, which, whilst living in This World, Wish to follow *the Nature of it*.' I could not help Smiling at the difference between the doctrines of Dr. Trusler & those of Christ. But, however, for his own sake I am sorry that a Man should be so enamour'd of Rowlandson's caricatures as to call them copies from life & manners, or fit Things for a Clergyman to write upon.

Pray let me intreat you to persevere in your Designing; it is the only source of Pleasure. All your other pleasures depend upon it. It is the Tree; your Pleasures are the Fruit. Your Inventions of Intellectual Visions are the Stamina of every thing you value. Go on, if not for your own sake, yet for ours, who love & admire your works; but, above all, For the Sake of the Arts. Do not throw aside for any long time the honour intended you by Nature to revive the Greek workmanship. I study your outlines as usual, just as if they were antiques.

As to Myself, about whom you are so kindly Interested, I live by Miracle. I am Painting small Pictures from the Bible. For as to Engraving, in which art I cannot reproach myself with any neglect, yet I am laid by in a corner as if I did not Exist, & Since my Young's Night Thoughts have been publish'd, Even Johnson & Fuseli have discarded my Graver. But as I know that He who Works & has his health cannot starve, I laugh at Fortune & Go on & on. I think I foresee better Things than I have ever seen. My Work pleases my employer, & I have an order for Fifty small Pictures at One Guinea each, which is Something better than mere copying after another artist. But above all, I feel myself happy & contented let what will come; having passed now near twenty years in ups & downs, I am used to them, & perhaps a little practise in them may turn out to benefit. It is now Exactly Twenty years since I was upon the ocean of business, & Tho' I laugh at Fortune, I am perswaded that She Alone is the Governor of Worldly Riches, & when it is Fit She will call on me; till then I wait with Patience, in hopes that She is busied among my Friends.

With Mine & My Wife's best compliments to Mrs. Cumberland, I remain,

Yours sincerely,

WILLM. BLAKE

To John Flaxman

(12th September, 1800.)

My Dearest Friend,

It is to you I owe All my present Happiness. It is to you I owe perhaps the Principal Happiness of my life. I have presum'd on your friendship in staying so long away & not calling to know of your welfare, but hope now every thing is nearly completed for our removal to Felpham, that I shall see you on Sunday, as we have appointed Sunday afternoon to call on Mrs. Flaxman at Hampstead. I send you a few lines, which I hope you will excuse. And As the time is arriv'd when Men shall again converse in Heaven & walk with Angels, I know you will be pleased with the Intention, & hope you will forgive the Poetry.

To My Dearest Friend, John Flaxman, these lines:

I bless thee, O Father of Heaven & Earth, that ever I saw Flaxman's face.

Angels stand round my Spirit in Heaven, the blessed of Heaven are my friends upon Earth.

When Flaxman was taken to Italy, Fuseli was given to me for a season,

And now Flaxman hath given me Hayley his friend to be mine, such my lot upon Earth.

Now my lot in the Heavens is this, Milton lov'd me in childhood & shew'd me his face.

Ezra came with Isaiah the Prophet, but Shakespeare in riper years gave me his hand;

Paracelsus & Behmen appear'd to me, terrors appear'd in
    the Heavens above
And in Hell beneath, & a mighty & awful change threatened
    the Earth.
The American War began. All its dark horrors passed before
    my face
Across the Atlantic to France. Then the French Revolution
    commenc'd in thick clouds,
And My Angels have told me that seeing such visions I
    could not subsist on the Earth,
But by my conjunction with Flaxman, who knows to forgive
    Nervous Fear.

        I remain, for Ever Yours,

            WILLIAM BLAKE.

Be so kind as to Read & then seal the Inclosed & send it on
its much beloved Mission.

To Thomas Butts

            (*Postmark* Sep. 23, 1800.)

Dear Friend of My Angels,

   We are safe arrived at our Cottage without accident or
hindrance, tho' it was between Eleven & Twelve O'Clock at
night before we could get home, owing to the necessary
shifting of our boxes & portfolios from one Chaise to another.
We had Seven different Chaises & as many different drivers.
All upon the road was chearfulness & welcome; tho' our
luggage was very heavy there was no grumbling at all. We
travel'd thro' a most beautiful country on a most glorious
day. Our Cottage is more beautiful than I thought it, & also
more convenient, for tho' small it is well proportion'd, & if I
should ever build a Palace it would be only My Cottage
Enlarged. Please to tell Mrs. Butts that we have dedicated a

Chamber for her service, & that it has a very fine view of the Sea. Mr. Hayley reciev'd me with his usual brotherly affection. My Wife & Sister are both very well, & courting Neptune for an Embrace, whose terrors this morning made them afraid, but whose mildness is often Equal to his terrors. The Villagers of Felpham are not meer Rustics; they are polite & modest. Meat is cheaper than in London, but the sweet air & the voices of winds, trees & birds, & the odours of the happy ground, makes it a dwelling for immortals. Work will go on here with God speed. – A roller & two harrows lie before my window. I met a plow on my first going out at my gate the first morning after my arrival, & the Plowboy said to the Plowman, 'Father, The Gate is Open.' – I have begun to Work, & find that I can work with greater pleasure than ever. Hope soon to give you a proof that Felpham is propitious to the Arts.

God bless you! I shall wish for you on Tuesday Evening as usual. Pray give My & My wife & sister's love & respects to Mrs. Butts; accept them yourself, & believe me for ever

Your affectionate & obliged Friend,

WILLIAM BLAKE.

My Sister will be in town in a week, & bring with her your account & whatever else I can finish.

Direct to Me:

Blake, Felpham, near Chichester, Sussex.

To William Hayley

Felpham, 26th November, 1800.

Dear Sir,

Absorbed by the poets Milton, Homer, Camoens, Ercilla, Ariosto, and Spenser, whose physiognomies have been my delightful study, *Little Tom* has been of late unattended to, and my wife's illness not being quite gone off, she has not printed any more since you went to London. But we can muster a few in colours and some in black, which I hope will be no less favour'd, tho' they are rough like rough sailors. We mean to begin printing again to-morrow. Time flies very fast and very merrily. I sometimes try to be miserable that I may do more work, but find it is a foolish experiment. Happinesses have wings and wheels; miseries are leaden legged, and their whole exployment is to clip the wings and to take off the wheels of our chariots. We determine, therefore, to be happy and do all that we can, tho' not all that we would. Our dear friend Flaxman is the theme of my emulation in this of industry, as well as in other virtues and merits. Gladly I hear of his full health and spirits. Happy son of the immortal Phidias, his lot is truly glorious, and mine no less happy in his friendship and in that of his friends. Our cottage is surrounded by the same guardians you left with us; they keep off every wind. We hear the west howl at a distance, the south bounds on high over our thatch, and smiling on our cottage says: 'You lay too low for my anger to injure.' As to the east and north, I believe they cannot get past the Turret.

My wife joins with me in duty and affection to you. Please to remember us both in love to Mr. and Mrs. Flaxman, and

believe me to be your affectionate,

Enthusiastic, hope-fostered visionary,

WILLIAM BLAKE.

To Thomas Butts

Felpham,
May 10, 1801.

My Dear Sir,

The necessary application to my Duty, as well to my old as new friends, has prevented me from that respect I owe in particular to you. And your accustomed forgiveness of my want of dexterity in certain points Emboldens me to hope that Forgiveness to be continued to me a little longer, When I shall be Enabled to throw off all obstructions to success.

Mr. Hayley acts like a Prince. I am at complete Ease, but I wish to do my duty, especially to you, who were the precursor of my present Fortune. I never will send you a picture unworthy of my present proficiency. I soon shall send you several; my present engagements are in Miniature Painting. Miniature is become a Goddess in my Eyes, & my Friends in Sussex say that I Excel in the pursuit. I have a great many orders, & they Multiply.

Now – let me intreat you to give me orders to furnish every accomodation in my power to recieve you & Mrs. Butts. I know my Cottage is too narrow for your Ease & comfort; we have one room in which we could make a bed to lodge you both, & if this is sufficient, it is at your service; but as beds & rooms & accomodations are easily procur'd by one on the spot, permit me to offer my service in either way, either in my cottage, or in a lod(g)ing in the village, as is most agreeable to you, if you & Mrs. Butts should think Bognor a pleasant relief from business in the Summer. It will give me the utmost delight to do my best.

Sussex is certainly a happy place, & Felpham in particular is the sweetest spot on Earth, at least it is so to me & My Good Wife, who desires her kindest Love to Mrs. Butts & yourself; accept mine also, & believe me to remain,

Your devoted,
WILL BLAKE.

To John Flaxman

Oct. 19, 1801.

Dear Flaxman,

I rejoice to hear that your Great Work is accomplish'd. Peace opens the way to greater still. The Kingdoms of this

World are now become the Kingdoms of God & his Christ, & we shall reign with him for ever & ever. The Reign of Literature & the Arts Commences. Blessed are those who are found studious of Literature & Humane & polite accomplishments. Such have their lamps burning & such shall shine as the stars.

Mr. Thomas, your friend to whom you was so kind as to make honourable mention of me, has been at Felpham & did me the favor to call on me. I have promis'd him to send my designs for Comus when I have done them, directed to you.

Now I hope to see the Great Works of Art, as they are so near to Felpham, Paris being scarce further off than London. But I hope that France & England will henceforth be as One Country and their Arts One, & that you will Ere long be erecting Monuments In Paris – Emblems of Peace.

My Wife joins with me in love to You & Mrs. Flaxman.

I remain, Yours Sincerely

WILLIAM BLAKE.

To Thomas Butts

Felpham,
Jany. 10, 1802.

Dear Sir,

Your very kind & affectionate Letter & the many kind things you have said in it, call'd upon me for an immediate answer; but it found My Wife & Myself so Ill, & My wife so very ill, that till now I have not been able to do this duty. The Ague & Rheumatism have been almost her constant Enemies, which she has combated in vain ever since we have been here; & her sickness is always my sorrow, of course. But what you tell me about your sight afflicted me not a little, & that about your health, in another part of your letter, makes me intreat you to take due care of both; it is a part of our duty to God & man to take due care of his Gifts; & tho' we ought not (to) think *more* highly of ourselves, yet we ought to think *As* highly of ourselves as immortals ought to think.

When I came down here, I was more sanguine than I am at present; but it was because I was ignorant of many things which have since occurred, & chiefly the unhealthiness of the place. Yet I do not repent of coming on a thousand accounts; & Mr. H., I doubt not, will do ultimately all that both he & I wish – that is, to lift me out of difficulty; but this is no easy matter to a man who, having Spiritual Enemies of such formidable magnitude, cannot expect to want natural hidden ones.

Your approbation of my pictures is a Multitude to Me, & I doubt not that all your kind wishes in my behalf shall in due time be fulfilled. Your kind offer of pecuniary assistance I can only thank you for at present, because I have enough to serve my present purpose here; our expenses are small, & our income, from our incessant labour, fully adequate to them at present. I am now engaged in Engraving 6 small plates for a New Edition of Mr. Hayley's Triumphs of Temper, from drawings by Maria Flaxman, sister to my friend the Sculptor, and it seems that other things will follow in course, if I do but Copy these well; but Patience! if Great things do not turn out, it is because such things depend on the Spiritual & not on the Natural World; & if it was fit for me, I doubt not that I should be Employ'd in Greater things; & when it is proper, my Talents shall be properly exercised in Public, as I hope they are now in private; for, till then, I leave no stone unturn'd & no path unexplor'd that tends to improvement in my beloved Arts. One thing of real consequence I have accomplish'd by coming into the country, which is to me consolation enough: namely, I have recollected all my scatter'd thoughts on Art & resumed my primitive & original ways of Execution in both painting & engraving which in the confusion of London I had very much lost & obliterated from my mind. But whatever becomes of my labours, I would rather that they should be preserv'd in your Green House (not, as you mistakenly call it, dung hill) than in the cold gallery of fashion.– The Sun may yet shine, & then they will be brought into open air.

But you have so generously & openly desired that I will divide my griefs with you, that I cannot hide what it is now become my duty to explain. – My unhappiness has arisen from a source which, if explor'd too narrowly, might hurt my pecuniary circumstances, As my dependence is on Engraving at present, & particularly on the Engravings I have in hand for Mr. H.: & I find on all hands great objections to my doing any thing but the meer drudgery of business, & intimations that if I do not confine myself to this, I shall not live; this has always pursu'd me. You will understand by this the source of all my uneasiness. This from Johnson & Fuseli brought me down here, & this from Mr. H. will bring me back again; for that I cannot live without doing my duty to lay up treasures in heaven is Certain & Determined, & to this I have long made up my mind, & why this should be made an objection to Me, while Drunkenness, Lewdness, Gluttony & even Idleness itself, does not hurt other men, let Satan himself Explain. The Thing I have most at Heart – more than life, or all that seems to make life comfortable without – Is the interest of True Religion & Science, & whenever any thing appears to affect that Interest (Especially if I myself omit any duty to my Station as a Soldier of Christ), It gives me the greatest of torments. I am not ashamed, afraid, or averse to tell you what Ought to be Told: That I am under the direction of Messengers from Heaven, Daily & Nightly; but the nature of such things is not, as some suppose, without trouble or care. Temptations are on the right hand & left; behind, the sea of time & space roars & follows swiftly; he who keeps not right onward is lost, & if our footsteps slide in clay, how can we do otherwise than fear & tremble? but I should not have troubled You with this account of my spiritual state, unless it had been necessary in explaining the actual cause of my uneasiness, into which you are so kind as to Enquire; for I never obtrude such things on others unless question'd, & then I never disguise the truth. – But if we fear to do the dictates of our Angels, & tremble at the Tasks set before us; if we refuse to do Spiritual Acts because of Natural Fears of Natural Desires! Who can describe the dismal torments of such a state! – I too well remember the Threats I heard! – If you, who are organised by Divine Providence for Spiritual communion, Refuse, & bury your Talent in the Earth, even tho' you should want Natural Bread, Sorrow & Desperation pursues you thro' life, & after death shame & confusion of face to eternity. Every one in Eternity will leave you, aghast at the Man who was crown'd with glory & honour by his brethren, & betray'd their cause to their enemies. You will be call'd the base Judas who betray'd his Friend! – Such words would make any stout man tremble, & how then could I be at ease? But I am now no longer in That State, & now go on again with my Task, Fearless, and tho' my path is difficult, I have no fear of stumbling while I keep it.

My wife desires her kindest Love to Mrs. Butts, & I have permitted her to send it to you also; we often wish that we could unite again in Society, & hope that the time is not distant when we shall do so, being determin'd not to remain another winter here, but to return to London.

I hear a voice you cannot hear, that says I must not stay,
I see a hand you cannot see, that beckons me away.

Naked we came here, naked of Natural things, & naked we shall return; but while cloth'd with the Divine Mercy, we are richly cloth'd in Spiritual & suffer all the rest gladly. Pray give my Love to Mrs. Butts & your family.

I am, Yours Sincerely,

WILLIAM BLAKE.

P.S. Your Obliging proposal of Exhibiting my two Pictures likewise calls for my thanks; I will finish the other, & then we shall judge of the matter with certainty.

To James Blake

Felpham,
Jany. 30, 1803.

Dear Brother,

Your Letter mentioning Mr. Butts' account of my Ague surprized me because I have no Ague, but have had a Cold this Winter. You know that it is my way to make the best of every thing. I never make myself nor my friends uneasy if I can help it. My Wife has had Agues & Rheumatisms almost ever since she has been here, but our time is almost out that we took the Cottage for. I did not mention our Sickness to you & should not to Mr. Butts but for a determination which we have lately made, namely To leave This Place, because I am now certain of what I have long doubted, Viz that H. is jealous as Stothard was & will be no further My friend than he is compell'd by circumstances. The truth is, As a Poet he is frighten'd at me & as a Painter his views & mine are opposite; he thinks to turn me into a Portrait Painter as he did Poor Romney, but this he nor all the devils in hell will never do. I must own that seeing H. like S., Envious (& that he is I am now certain) made me very uneasy, but it is over & I now defy the worst & fear

not while I am true to myself which I will be. This is the
uneasiness I spoke of to Mr. Butts, but I did not tell him so
plain & wish you to keep it a secret & to burn this letter
because it speaks so plain. I told Mr. Butts that I did not
wish to Explore too much the cause of our determination to
leave Felpham because of pecuniary connexions between
H. & me – Be not then uneasy on any account & tell my
Sister not to be uneasy, for I am fully Employ'd & Well
Paid. I have made it so much H's interest to employ me that
he can no longer treat me with indifference & now it is in
my power to stay or return or remove to any other place
that I choose, because I am getting before hand in money
matters. The Profits arising from Publication are immense,
& I now have it in my power to commence publication
with many very formidable works, which I have finish'd &
ready. A Book price half a guinea may be got out at the
Expense of Ten pounds & its almost certain profits are
500 G. I am only sorry that I did not know the methods of
publishing years ago, & this is one of the numerous benefits
I have obtain'd by coming here, for I should never have
known the nature of Publication unless I had known H. &
his connexions & his method of managing. It now would be
folly not to venture publishing. I am now Engraving Six
little plates for a little work of Mr. H's, for which I am to
have 10 Guineas each, & the certain profits of that work are
a fortune such as would make me independent, supposing
that I could substantiate such a one of my own & I mean to
try many. But I again say as I said before, We are very
Happy sitting at tea by a wood fire in our Cottage, the wind
singing above our roof & the sea roaring at a distance, but
if sickness comes all is unpleasant.

But my letter to Mr. Butts appears to me not to be so
explicit as that to you, for I told you that I should come to
London in the Spring to commence Publisher & he has
offer'd me every assistance in his power without knowing

my intention. But since I wrote yours we had made the resolution of which we inform'd him, viz to leave Felpham entirely. I also told you what I was about & that I was not ignorant of what was doing in London in works of art. But I did not mention Illness because I hoped to get better (for I was really very ill when I wrote to him the last time) & was not then perswaded as I am now that the air tho' warm is unhealthy.

However, this I know will set you at Ease. I am now so full of work that I have had no time to go on with the Ballads, & my prospects of more & more work continually are certain. My Heads of Cowper for Mr. H's life of Cowper have pleas'd his Relations exceedingly & in Particular Lady Hesketh & Lord Cowper – to please Lady H. was a doubtful chance who almost ador'd her Cousin the poet & thought him all perfection, & she writes that she is quite satisfied with the portraits & charm'd by the great Head in particular, tho' she never could bear the original Picture.

But I ought to mention to you that our present idea is: To take a house in some village further from the Sea, Perhaps Lavant, & in or near the road to London for the sake of convenience. I also ought to inform you that I read your letter to Mr. H. & that he is very afraid of losing me & also very afraid that my Friends in London should have a bad opinion of the reception he has given to me. But My Wife has undertaken to Print the whole number of the Plates for Cowper's work, which she does to admiration, & being under my own eye the prints are as fine as the French prints & please every one: in short I have Got every thing so under my thumb that it is more profitable that things should be as they are than any other way, tho' not so agreeable, because we wish naturally for friendship in preference to interest.– The Publishers are already indebted to My Wife Twenty Guineas for work deliver'd; this is a small specimen of how we go on: then fear nothing & let my Sister fear nothing because it appears to me that I am now too old & have had too much experience to be any longer imposed upon, only illness makes all uncomfortable & this we must prevent by every means in our power.

I send with this 5 Copies of N4 of the Ballads for Mrs. Flaxman & Five more, two of which you will be so good as to give to Mrs. Chetwynd if she should call or send for them. These Ballads are likely to be Profitable, for we have Sold all that we have had time to print. Evans the Bookseller in Pall-mall says they go off very well, & why should we repent of having done them? it is doing Nothing that is to be repented of & not doing such things as these.

Pray remember us both to Mr. Hall when you see him.

I write in great haste & with a head full of botheration about various projected works & particularly a work now Proposed to the Public at the End of Cowper's Life, which will very likely be of great consequence; it is Cowper's Milton, the same that Fuseli's Milton Gallery was painted for, & if we succeed in our intentions the prints to this work will be very profitable to me & not only profitable, but honourable at any rate. The Project pleases Lord Cowper's family, & I am now labouring in my thoughts Designs for this & other works equally creditable. These are works to be boasted of, & therefore I cannot feel depress'd, tho' I know that as far as Designing & Poetry are concern'd I am Envied in many Quarters, but I will cram the dogs, for I know that the Public are my friends & love my works & will embrace them whenever they see them. My only Difficulty is to produce fast enough.

I go on Merrily with my Greek & Latin; am very sorry that I did not begin to learn languages early in life as I find it very Easy; am now learning my Hebrew אבנ. I read Greek as fluently as an Oxford scholar & the Testament is my chief master: astonishing indeed is the English

Translation, it is almost word for word, & if the Hebrew Bible is as well translated, which I do not doubt it is, we need not doubt of its having been translated as well as written by the Holy Ghost:

my wife joins me in Love to you both.

I am,

Sincerely yours,

W. BLAKE.

Memorandum

In Refutation of 'The Information and Complaint of John Scholfield, a Private Soldier'

(August, 1803.)

The Soldier has been heard to say repeatedly, that he did not know how the Quarrel began, which he would not say if such seditious words were spoken.

Mrs. Haynes Evidences, that she saw me turn him down the Road, & all the while we were at the Stable Door, and that not one word of charge against me was uttered, either relating to Sedition or any thing else; all he did was swearing and threatening.

Mr. Hosier heard him say that he would be revenged, and would have me hanged if he could: He spoke this the Day after my turning him out of the Garden. Hosier says he is ready to give Evidence of this, if necessary.

The Soldier's Comrade swore before the Magistrates, while I was present, that he heard me utter seditious words, at the Stable Door, and in particular, said, that he heard me D – the K – g. Now I have all the Persons who were present at the Stable Door to witness that no Word relating to Seditious Subjects was uttered, either by one party or the other, and they are ready, on their Oaths, to say that I did not utter such Words.

Mrs. Haynes says very sensibly, that she never heard

People quarrel, but they always charged each other with the Offence, and repeated it to those around, therefore as the Soldier charged not me with Seditious Words at that Time, neither did his Comrade, the whole Charge must have been fabricated in the Stable afterwards.

If we prove the Comrade perjured who swore that he heard me D – the K – g, I believe the whole Charge falls to the Ground.

Mr. Cosens, owner of the Mill at Felpham, was passing by in the Road, and saw me and the Soldier and William standing near each other; he heard nothing, but says we certainly were not quarrelling.

The whole Distance that William could be at any Time of the Conversation between me and the Soldier (supposing such Conversation to have existed) is only 12 Yards, & W – says that he was backwards and forwards in the Garden. It was a still Day, there was no Wind stirring.

William says on his Oath, that the first Words that he heard me speak to the Soldier were ordering him out of the Garden; the truth is, I did not speak to the Soldier till then, & my ordering him out of the Garden was occasioned by his saying something that I thought insulting.

The Time that I & the Soldier were together in the Garden was not sufficient for me to have uttered the Things that he alledged.

The Soldier said to Mrs. Grinder, that it would be right to have my House searched, as I might have Plans of the Country which I intended to send to the Enemy; he called me a Military Painter; I suppose mistaking the Words Miniature Painter, which he might have heard me called. I think that this proves, his having come into the Garden with some bad Intention, or at least with a prejudiced Mind.

It is necessary to learn the Names of all that were present at the Stable Door, that we may not have any Witnesses brought against us, that were not there.

All the Persons present at the Stable Door were, Mrs. Grinder and her Daughter, all the Time; Mrs. Haynes & her Daughter all the Time; Mr. Grinder, part of the Time; Mr. Hayley's Gardener part of the Time. – Mrs. Haynes was present from my turning him out at my Gate, all the rest of the Time. What passed in the Garden, there is no Person but William & the Soldier, & myself can know.

There was not any body in Grinder's Tap-room, but an Old Man, named Jones, who (Mrs. Grinder says) did not come out. He is the same Man who lately hurt his Hand, & wears it in a sling.

The Soldier after he and his Comrade came together into the Tap-room, threatened to knock William's Eyes out (this was his often repeated Threat to me and to my Wife) because W – refused to go with him to Chichester, and swear against me. William said that he would not take a false Oath, for that he heard me say nothing of the Kind (i.e. Sedition) Mr. Grinder then reproved the Soldier for threatening William, and Mr. Grinder said, that W – should not go, because of those Threats, especially as he was sure that no seditious Words were spoken.

William's timidity in giving his Evidence before the Magistrates, and his fear of uttering a Falsehood upon Oath, proves him to be an honest Man, & is to me an host of Strength. I am certain that if I had not turned the Soldier out of my Garden, I never should have been free from his Impertinence & Intrusion.

Mr. Hayley's Gardener came past at the Time of the Contention at the Stable Door, & going to the Comrade said to him, Is your Comrade drunk? – a Proof that he thought the Soldier abusive, & in an Intoxication of Mind.

If such a Perjury as this can take effect, any Villain in future may come & drag me and my Wife out of our House, & beat us in the Garden, or use us as he please, or is able, & afterwards go and swear our Lives away.

Is it not in the Power of any Thief who enters a Man's Dwelling, & robs him, or misuses his Wife or Children, to go & swear as this Man has sworn.

To William Hayley

London,
October 7, 1803.

Dear Sir,

Your generous & tender solicitude about your devoted rebel makes it absolutely necessary that he should trouble you with an account of his safe arrival, which will excuse his begging the favor of a few lines to inform him how you escaped the contagion of the Court of Justice – I fear that you have & must suffer more on my account than I shall ever be worth – Arrived safe in London, my wife in very poor health, still I resolve not to lose hope of seeing better days.

Art in London flourishes. Engravers in particular are wanted. Every Engraver turns away work that he cannot execute from his superabundant Employment. Yet no one brings work to me. I am content that it shall be so as long as God pleases. I know that many works of a lucrative nature are in want of hands; other Engravers are courted. I suppose that I must go a Courting, which I shall do awkwardly; in the mean time I lose no moment to complete Romney to satisfaction.

How is it possible that a Man almost 50 Years of Age, who has not lost any of his life since he was five years old without incessant labour & study, how is it possible that such a one with ordinary common sense can be inferior to a boy of twenty, who scarcely has taken or deigns to take a pencil in hand, but who rides about the Parks or Saunters about the Playhouses, who Eats & drinks for business not for need, how is it possible that such a fop can be superior to the studious lover of Art can scarcely be imagin'd. Yet such is somewhat like my fate & such it is likely to remain. Yet I laugh & sing, for if on Earth neglected I am in heaven a Prince among Princes, & even on Earth beloved by the Good as a Good Man; this I should be perfectly contented with, but at certain periods a blaze of reputation arises round me in which I am consider'd as one distinguish'd by some mental perfection, but the flame soon dies again & I am left stupified and astonish'd. O that I could live as others do in a regular succession of Employment, this wish I fear is not to be accomplish'd to me – Forgive this Dirge-like lamentation over a dead horse, & now I have lamented over the dead horse let me laugh & be merry with my friends till Christmas, for as Man liveth not by bread alone, I shall live altho' I should want bread – nothing is necessary to me but to do my Duty & to rejoice in the exceeding joy that is always poured out on my Spirit, to pray that my friends & you above the rest may be made partakers of the joy that the world cannot concieve, that you may still be replenish'd with the same & be as you always have been, a glorious & triumphant Dweller in immortality. Please to pay for me my best thanks to Miss Poole: tell her that I wish her a continued Excess of Happiness – some say that Happiness is not Good for Mortals, & they ought to be answer'd that Sorrow is not fit for Immortals & is utterly useless to any one; a blight never does good to a tree, & if a blight kill not a tree but it still bear fruit, let none say that the fruit was in consequence of the blight. When this Soldier-like danger is over I will do double the work I do now, for it will hang heavy on my Devil who terribly resents it; but I soothe him to peace, & indeed he is a good natur'd Devil after all & certainly does not lead me into scrapes – he is not in the least to be blamed for the present scrape, as he was out of the way all the time on other employment seeking amusement in making Verses, to which he constantly leads me very much to my hurt & sometimes to the annoyance of my friends; as I percieve he is now doing the same work by my letter, I will finish it, wishing you health & joy in God our Saviour.

> To Eternity yours,
> WILLM. BLAKE.

To Richard Phillips

> 17 Sth Molton St.
> Oct 14 (1807)

Sir,

A circumstance has occurred which has again raised my Indignation.

I read in the Oracle & True Briton of Octr. 13, 1807, that a Mr. Blair, a Surgeon, has, *with the Cold fury of Robespierre,* caused the Police to sieze upon the Person & Goods or Property of an Astrologer & to commit him to Prison. The Man who can Read the Stars often is opressed by their Influence, no less than the Newtonian who reads Not & cannot Read is opressed by his own Reasonings & Experiments. We are all subject to Error: Who shall say, Except the Natural Religionists, that we are not all subject to Crime?

My desire is that you would Enquire into this Affair & that you would publish this in your Monthly Magazine. I do not pay the postage of this Letter, because you, as Sheriff, are bound to attend to it.

> WILLIAM BLAKE.

To Josiah Wedgwood

17 South Molton Street,
8 Septembr., 1815.

Sir,

I send Two more drawings with the First that I did, altered, having taken out that part which expressed the hole for the ladle.

It will be more convenient to me to make all the drawings first, before I begin Engraving them, as it will enable me also to regulate a System of working that will be uniform from beginning to end. Any Remarks that you may be pleased to make will be thankfully reciev'd by, Sir

Your humble Servant

WILLIAM BLAKE.

To John Linnell

Feby. 1, 1826.

Dear Sir,

I am forced to write, because I cannot come to you, & this on two accounts. First, I omitted to desire you would come & take a Mutton chop with us the day you go to Cheltenham, & I will go with you to the Coach; also, I will go to Hampstead to see Mrs. Linnell on Sunday, but will return before dinner (I mean if you set off before that), & Second, I wish to have a Copy of Job to shew to Mr. Chantr(e)y.

For I am again laid up by a cold in my stomach; the Hampstead Air, as it always did, so I fear it always will do this, Except it be the Morning air; & That, in my Cousin's time, I found I could bear with safety & perhaps benefit. I believe my Constitution to be a good one, but it has many peculiarities that no one but myself can know. When I was young, Hampstead, Highgate, Hornsea, Muswell Hill, & even Islington & all places North of London, always laid me up the day after, & sometimes two or three days, with precisely the same Complaint & the same torment of the Stomach, Easily removed, but excruciating while it lasts & enfeebling for some time after. Sr. Francis Bacon would say, it is want of discipline in Mountainous Places. Sr. Francis Bacon is a Liar. No discipline will turn one Man into another, even in the least particle, & such discipline I call Presumption & Folly. I have tried it too much not to know this, & am very sorry for all such who may be led to such ostentatious Exertion against their Eternal Existence itself, because it is Mental Rebellion against the Holy Spirit, & fit only for a Soldier of Satan to perform.

Though I hope in a morning or two to call on you in Cirencester Place, I feared you might be gone, or I might be too ill to let you know how I am, & what I wish.

I am, dear Sir,

Yours Sincerely,

WILLIAM BLAKE.

To John Linnell

February, 1827.

Dear Sir,

I thank you for the Five Pounds recieved to day: am getting better every Morning, but slowly, as I am still feeble & tottering, tho' all the Symptoms of my complaint seem almost gone as the fine weather is very beneficial & comfortable to me. I go on, as I think, improving my Engravings of Dante more & more, & shall soon get Proofs of these Four which I have, & beg the favour of you to send me the two Plates of Dante which you have, that I may finish them sufficiently to make some shew of Colour & Strength.

I have thought & thought of the Removal & cannot get my Mind out of a state of terrible fear at such a step; the more I think, the more I feel terror at what I wish'd at first & thought it a thing of benefit & Good hope; you will attribute it to its right Cause—Intellectual Peculiarity, that must be Myself alone shut up in Myself, or Reduced to Nothing. I could tell you of Visions & dreams upon the Subject. I have asked & intreated Divine help, but fear continues upon me, & I must relinquish the step that I had wish'd to take, & still wish, but in vain.

Your Success in your Profession is above all things to me most gratifying; may it go on to the Perfection you wish & more. So wishes also

Yours Sincerely,
WILLIAM BLAKE.

To George Cumberland

N 3, Fountain Court, Strand.

12 April, 1827.

Dear Cumberland,

I have been very near the Gates of Death & have returned very weak & an Old Man feeble & tottering, but not in Spirit & Life, not in The Real Man The Imagination which Liveth for Ever. In that I am stronger & stronger as this Foolish Body decays. I thank you for the Pains you have taken with Poor Job. I know too well that a great majority of Englishmen are fond of The Indefinite which they Measure by Newton's Doctrine of the Fluxions of an Atom, A Thing that does not Exist. These are Politicians & think that Republican Art is Inimical to their Atom. For a Line or

Lineament is not formed by Chance: a Line is a Line in its Minutest Subdivisions: Strait or Crooked It is Itself & Not Intermeasurable with or by any Thing Else. Such is Job, but since the French Revolution Englishmen are all Intermeasurable One by Another, Certainly a happy state of Agreement to which I for One do not Agree. God keep me from the Divinity of Yes & No too, The Yea Nay Creeping Jesus, from supposing Up & Down to be the same Thing as all Experimentalists must suppose.

You are desirous I know to dispose of some of my Works & to make them Pleasin(g). I am obliged to you & to all who do so. But having none remaining of all that I had Printed I cannot Print more Except at a great loss, for at the time I printed those things I had a whole House to range in: now I am shut up in a Corner therefore am forced to ask a Price for them that I scarce expect to get from a Stranger. I am now Printing a Set of the Songs of Innocence & Experience for a Friend at Ten Guineas which I cannot do under Six Months consistent with my other Work, so that I have little hope of doing any more of such things. The Last Work I produced is a Poem Entitled Jerusalem the Emanation of the Giant Albion, but find that to Print it will Cost my Time the amount of Twenty Guineas. One I have Finish'd. It contains 100 Plates but it is not likely that I shall get a Customer for it.

As you wish me to send you a list with the Prices of these things they are as follows

	£.	s.	d.
America	6	6	0
Europe	6	6	0
Visions &c	5	5	0
Thel	3	3	0
Songs of Inn. & Exp.	10	10	0
Urizen	6	6	0

The Little Card I will do as soon as Possible but when you Consider that I have been reduced to a Skeleton from which I am slowly recovering you will I hope have Patience with me.

Flaxman is Gone & we must All soon follow, every one to his Own Eternal House, Leaving the Delusive Goddess Nature & her Laws to get into Freedom from all Law of the Members into The Mind, in which every one is King & Priest in his own House. God send it so on Earth as it is in Heaven.

I am, Dear Sir, Yours Affectionately

WILLIAM BLAKE.

INDEX OF FIRST LINES

MORE ABOUT PENGUINS
AND PELICANS

Penguinews, which appears every month, contains details of all the new books issued by Penguins as they are published. From time to time it is supplemented by *Penguins in Print*, which is our complete list of almost 5,000 titles.

A specimen copy of *Penguinews* will be sent to you free on request. Please write to Dept EP, Penguin Books Ltd, Harmondsworth, Middlesex, for your copy.

In the U.S.A.: For a complete list of books available from Penguins in the United States write to Dept CS, Penguin Books Inc., 7110 Ambassador Road, Baltimore, Maryland 21207.

In Canada: For a complete list of books available from Penguins in Canada write to Penguin Books Canada Ltd, 41 Steelcase Road West, Markham, Ontario.

Children of Albion

POETRY OF 'THE UNDERGROUND' IN BRITAIN

Here at last is the 'secret' generation of more or less British poets whose work could hitherto be discovered only through their own bush telegraph of little magazines and lively readings. These are the energies which have almost completely dispelled the arid critical climate of the fifties and engineered a fresh renaissance of 'the voice of the Bard' –

The anthology contains many of the best poems of

Pete Brown	Dave Cunliffe	Roy Fisher
Lee Harwood	Spike Hawkins	Anselm Hollo
Bernard Kops	Tom McGrath	Adrian Mitchell
Edwin Morgan	Neil Oram	Tom Pickard
Tom Raworth	Chris Torrance	Alex Trocchi
Gael Turnbull		

– and forty-seven others – from John Arden to Michael X

It is edited by Michael Horovitz, with a Blakean cornucopia of 'afterwords' which trace the development of oral and jazz poetry – the Albert Hall Incarnation of 1965 – the influences of the great American and Russian spokesmen – and the diverse lyric, (a) political, visioning and revolutionary orientations of these new poets – stretching out of the parochial slumber of old new lines towards the international and archetypal mainstreams of the word.

Poet to Poet

The response of one poet to the work of another can be doubly illuminating. In each volume of this new Penguin series a living poet presents his own edition of the work of a British or American poet of the past. By their choice of poet, by their selection of verses, and by the personal and critical reactions they express in their introductions, the poets of today thus provide an intriguing insight into themselves and their own work whilst reviving interest in poetry they have particularly admired.

Already published:

Crabbe by C. Day Lewis
Henryson by Hugh MacDiarmid
Herbert by W. H. Auden
Tennyson by Kingsley Amis
Wordsworth by Lawrence Durrell
Whitman by Robert Creeley
Jonson by Thom Gunn
Pope by Peter Levi
Shelley by Kathleen Raine

Future volumes will include:

Arnold by Stephen Spender
Marvell by William Empson
Wyatt by Allen Tate